Visions OF GLOBAL AMERICA AND THE FUTURE OF Critical Reading

Visions OF GLOBAL AMERICA AND THE FUTURE OF Critical Reading

DANIEL T. O'HARA

THE OHIO STATE UNIVERSITY PRESS
COLUMBUS

Copyright © 2009 by The Ohio State University.
All rights reserved.

Library of Congress Cataloging-in-Publication Data
O'Hara, Daniel T., 1948–
Visions of global America and the future of critical reading / Daniel T. O'Hara.
    p. cm.
Includes bibliographical references and index.
ISBN 978-0-8142-1104-5 (cloth : alk. paper)—ISBN 978-0-8142-9202-0 (cd-rom)
1. Criticism—United States. 2. American literature—History and criticism. 3. Truth.
4. Badiou, Alain—Criticism and interpretation. 5. Emerson, Ralph Waldo, 1803–1882—Criticism and interpretation. 6. James, Henry, 1843–1916—Criticism and interpretation.
7. Baldwin, James, 1924–1987—Criticism and interpretation. 8. Purdy, James—Criticism and interpretation. I. Title.
   PS55.037 2009
   801.'950973—dc22
                                      2009020642

This book is available in the following editions:
Cloth (ISBN 978-0-8142-1104-5)
CD-ROM (ISBN 978-0-8142-9202-0)
Paper (ISBN: 978-0-8142-5669-5)
Cover design by Juliet Williams
Type set in Adobe Sabon

contents

Preface — vii

Acknowledgments — xiii

Introduction The Event of Reading — 1

PART ONE: THE CRITICAL APPARATUS

1. Badiou's Truth and the Office of the Critic:
   Neither Gods nor Monsters — 15
2. Figures of the Void:
   On the Subject of Truth and the Fundamentalist Imagination — 38
3. "The Cry of Its Occasion":
   The Subject of Truth, Or the Terror in Global Terrorism — 55

PART TWO: THE LITERARY CULTURE OF GLOBAL AMERICA

4. Global America and the Logics of Vision — 73
5. America, the Symptom:
   On the Post-9/11 Allegory in American Studies — 81
6. Our Worldly Apocalypse:
   Literature and Everyday Life — 97

PART THREE: THE EXALTED STATES OF READING

7. "Monstrous Levity":
   Between Realism and Vision in Henry James — 111
8. Toward a Global Democracy:
   James Baldwin and the Stoic Vision of *Amor Fati* — 120
9. Bringing Out the Terror:
   James Purdy and the Culture of Vision — 132

CONTENTS

Conclusion The Truth of American Madness:
            On Love and Vision in *The Golden Bowl*   150

Appendix   Why Badiou Counts—In This Book and Generally   161
Notes   165
Index   175

preface

> She went in silence to where her friend—never in intention visibly so much her friend as at that moment—had braced herself to so amazing an energy, and there under Amerigo's eyes she picked up the shinning pieces. Bedizened and jeweled, in her rustling finery, she paid, with humility of attitude, this prompt tribute to order—only to find however that she could carry but two of the fragments at once. She brought them over to the chimney-piece, to the conspicuous place occupied by the cup before Fanny's appropriation of it, and after laying them carefully down went back to what remained, the solid detached foot. With this she returned to the mantel-shelf, placing it with deliberation in the centre and then for a minute occupying herself as with the attempt to fit the other morsels together. The split determined by the latent crack was so sharp and so neat that if there had been anything to hold them the bowl might still quite beautifully, a few steps away, have passed for uninjured. As there was however nothing to hold them but Maggie's hands during the few moments the latter were so employed, she could only lay the almost equal parts of the vessel carefully beside their pedestal and leave them thus before her husband's eyes. . . . She had taken him for aware all day (that she *knew*); but what had been wrong about was the effect of his anxiety. . . . [I]t was shut there between them, the successive moments throbbing under it the while as the pulse of fever throbs under the doctor's thumb? (James, *The Golden Bowl* 435–36)[1]

How do we learn to read such a complex passage as this? How do we recognize and address its rich and various contexts? Perhaps most important: in our emerging "post-human" global society, what is there to be gained from such an experience of reading? That is the subject of this book. The final chapter of this book is intended to demonstrate the inter-animating experience of reading such a passage; the intervening chapters are the ways in which I have learned how to do it. For a more detailed account of my argument and the book's organization, please see the introduction.

For convenience, I have organized these chapters into three parts: "The Critical Apparatus," "The Literary Culture of Global America," and "The Exalted States of Reading." By elaborating the framework of part 1 through a continuing analysis of contemporary fundamentalism, I also implicitly discuss the sublime experiences of reading that is possible for the culture of global America.

Similarly, my introductory and concluding chapters explore and complete the book's theoretical agenda. The interrelationship of the book's parts is thus deliberate, as the reading entailed by passages such as that cited above require just that brand of interpenetrative process of textual *self-interpretation* I recommend. As good critical readers, I believe that we discover the truth of reading, in reading.

The essential premise of this book is that there is indeed an American difference to reading. In saying this, I do not assume that this difference lies in the optimistic and chauvinistic versions of American exceptionalism and manifest destiny, nor do I accept that identity politics are necessary or sufficient to the human condition in the early twenty-first century. Quite the contrary: I believe the American difference entails the specific dream of the human being transcending itself here *on this continent* in accordance with the romantic visionary desire for spiritual and material apotheosis. As such, this American dream is a terrible contingent nightmare for the rest of the human species, as well as for most of the other species on the planet. In this admittedly hyperbolic light, Mormonism, with its doctrine of eternal progression to divinity, is the most American of religions in our global American empire. An American Christian fundamentalism, on the other hand, claims that only the quality of one's personal relationship with Jesus warrants a free trip to heaven, all the while allowing the practice of a radical antinomianism here below.

The first chapter argues that the way this traditional romantic American version of liberated human nature plays itself out today is via the seductions of the post-human imagination. In this chapter, I marshal Alain Badiou's theory of truth and its implications for the transformative role of the critic in the face of such strong allures. While I admit that the post-human includes both popular sci-fi representations and scientific innovations that are making human biogenetic engineering increasingly possible, this book deals exclusively with the former. Since the mid-1970s, America has become a sci-fi culture, while those of us who are human (all-too-human) are living in poverty on, what I call, after Badiou, the edge of the void of representation.

Chapter 2 continues the elaboration of Badiou's militant theory of truth in relationship to what looks, at first blush, a lot like it—the contemporary fundamentalist imagination. What I point out here, however, is that where Badiou's militant truth is put to the test by its very own subject, the experience of fundamentalism better resembles what Freud recognized in the Schreber case: namely, that the psychotic mind can recover part of its balance in the mad myths to which it publicly testifies, regardless of their falsifiability. By using Badiou to analyze a specific case of the fundamentalist imagination in this chapter, I demonstrate what I call the American madness at work, even as I separate the experience of the authentic subject of truth from the profoundly self-deceived.

The final chapter of this first part on the critical framework of the book completes the elaboration of Badiou's theory of truth in a relationship to global terrorism and the source of the terror in its threat, especially after 9/11. It is here that the Lacanian dimension of my critical framework emerges more fully. Here I examine how and why the American subject must both disavow ever being split, while at the same time taking the most elaborate steps to repair the damage of that disavowed split. In the context of 9/11, the traditionally dominant forms of American culture have enacted this battle explicitly, but the structure of this struggle has been pervasive in American culture even before the event. The psychotic anxiety of this schizoid situation of disavowal and identification is the defining trauma of being an American; it is the real of American culture, and it has been confirmed with a vengeance by contemporary history.

Part 2, "The Literary Culture of Global America," lays out why and how this is the case. In chapter 4, I analyze the logics of the American visionary experience with respect to two representative cases of these logics at work: Ralph Waldo Emerson and Henry James. Emerson, whatever else he contains, espouses a vision whose logic makes a virtue of the incapacity to love by promising an apocalyptic self-transformation—a rebirth of self as a creative genius, even an apotheosis into a divinity—all in the name of Emerson's vision of "the new, yet unapproachable America." James writes consistently against this romantic vision of creativity, dramatizing the limits of the imagination, what he calls (in "The Middle of the Journey") "the infirmity of art," in "the candour of affection," an often tragically impossible love expressed best, most fully, in the parent-child relationship and its diverse avatars (347).[2]

Chapter 5 then discusses how the catachresis of "America," the metaphorical figure of America, plays both a symptomatic role in contemporary American studies, and can be made to play the role of what Lacan in his late work calls "*le sinthome.*" I reference James's "The Beast in the Jungle" to show how the symptom of the protagonist's fundamental incapacity for love can become, for James and his reader, a material thread of jouissance that animates and enhances their identity beyond gender or sexuality in the service of a truth of an ultimate impersonal intimacy—a prophetic vision by James of Lacan's *le sinthome.* My chapters on James Purdy and James's *The Golden Bowl* conduct similar experiments in critical reading to work out more fully how through self-reading we may transform what threatens our psychic dissolution into that which holds ourselves together.

Chapter 6 closes out part 2 by suggesting how reading for *le sinthome* so as to discover the subject of truth, amidst the (self-)terrorizing experience of the real, is in fact best accomplished by the art of reading as practiced by philology, especially as performed by Erich Auerbach. By taking this brand of reading to two literary texts of the 1970s, John Cheever's *Falconer* (1977) and John Ashbery's *Self-Portrait in a Convex Mirror* (1975), the theory of reading as the truth event of the modern split subject's self-recognition here connects Badiou on truth and Lacan on *le sinthome* with Auerbach on "*Ansatzpunckten*" and Hans Ulrich Gumbrecht's notion of "*Stimmung.*" To put this chapter's argument in a nutshell, as it were: just as "global America" is the catachresis for the emergence of an unprecedented modern form of imaginative hegemonic empire, so these terms of philological art provide an instance of the unprecedented event of reading my theory proposes and asks contemporary critical practice to perform.

Part 3 focuses on three forms of sublime (but not divine) exaltation in and through self-reading, in which reading is explicitly highlighted as such. Chapter 7 uses two artist-tales by Henry James to bring out the self-destructive experience of radical jouissance as the legacy of the Emersonian tradition. Chapter 8 then shows how Foucault's *The Hermeneutics of the Subject* recasts the Stoic vision of *amor fati* so that we may see it creatively repeated in James Baldwin's surprisingly Jamesian vision of the democracy of love as the best—most authentic—future of humanity. And chapter 9, putting into play to the fullest the Lacanian vision of the real and *le sinthome,* then argues that the vision of the subject in James Purdy's work is one where human subjectivity may be legitimately sacrificed in a self-overcoming unto death that testifies to the strength, not the weakness, of being human, and so gives the ultimate lie to global America and its grandiose post-human phantasms.

The book's conclusion then provides the reading promised by the preface. It gives the truth of the American madness that my reading of *The Golden Bowl*—made possible through the progress in reading of this book—would critique and temper via the "tough love" of James's tragic vision of life.

acknowledgments

Portions of chapters in this book started as unpublished lectures or published essays. I am grateful to my hosts and to the editors of *boundary 2* and *The Henry James Review* for permission to reprint them in their revised forms in this book.

introduction

THE EVENT OF READING

AS I WAS teaching "Introduction to Graduate Studies" recently, I noticed a passage in Erich Auerbach's *Mimesis* that has not previously attracted much attention. Auerbach is in the midst of sketching a popular post-romantic reading of the relationship between Don Quixote and Sancho Panza ("He had fallen in love with his master's madness and his own role," etc.), effectively tying Quixote and Panza to a long tradition of comic types from the ancient to the present.[1]

But then Auerbach suddenly interrupts himself. However much he feels the allure of this rather amateurish and popular perspective, Auerbach ruefully admits that since "the romantics" especially, "many things have been read into [Cervantes] which he hardly foreboded, let alone intended" (353). *Don Quixote*, Auerbach notes, has become iconic for its culture; it "dissociates itself from the author's intention and leads a life of its own." He sternly continues the passage: "Don Quixote shows a new face to every age which enjoys him. Yet the historian—whose task it is to define the place of a given work in a historical continuity—must endeavor, insofar as that is still possible, to attain a clear understanding of what the work meant to its author and his contemporaries" (353–54). The intellectual conscience of the good processional philologist here trumps the affective identification of the amateur.

This clear split between the amateur and the professional mirrors other splits in *Mimesis*. In the famous opening chapter, "Odysseus'

1

Scar," there is the split between the classical aesthetic of a seamless and decorous representation of the present moment in the heroic life of an aristocratic class versus the Hebraic evocation of something more in the mixture of styles, of mysterious gaps and ellipses of every life of a God-intoxicated people. There is a similar split performed in "The Brown Stocking," the (almost as famous) closing chapter on Virginia Woolf. Here the split lies between the deadly homogenizing trends of an emerging one-dimensional postwar world order (whether American or Soviet style is naturally not yet clear to Auerbach) and the exquisitely animating sublimities of the random moment of everyday life. The amateur, the Hebraic, and the radically contingent versus the professional and the classical and the rationalizing new order are the three sets of splits in the subject of reading that Auerbach's great work enacts before the reader's eyes. Each set is allusively associated with the extreme political representations of the liberal social democracies recently triumphant in the Second World War and the infamous, defeated Nazi state. Auerbach, in exile in Turkey for his Jewishness, has a big stake in these splits, especially the last.

I argued in my class, and contend here, that these explicit splits, as formulated by Auerbach more than sixty years ago, still haunt the subject of reading today. (The pause Auerbach's text gives me testifies to my own or any reader's truth event.) These splits have, of course, changed somewhat, but their presence is readily recognizable in the worldly conditions that face us now as critics. How we each line up with respect to these three homologous sets of splits varies considerably.

These critical self-oppositions—of amateur and professional, of classical decorum and sublime aesthetic experimentation, of radical contingency and instrumental reason—too often encourage a vicious circle of reading. We are unable to synthesize their reconciliation, unlike, we believe, in earlier epochs in Western cultural history such as the late Renaissance, the Enlightenment, and the Romantic Age. We currently disbelieve in even the possibility, or perhaps the desirability, of any such totalizing dialectical resolution. Preferring instead the free play of a postmodern situation without grand narratives, we wander and drift. We are creatures of the critical fashion of the moment, hoping for little more than inspiration to at least go on, for a while, a bit longer, like characters out of a bad parody of a Beckett play.

There is a more cheerful, heroically pessimistic way of viewing the divided modern subject of reading. Nietzsche, as Pierre Klossowski argues, pursues experimentally, via his so-called aphoristic and perspectivist style, the moment of self-division, like that in Auerbach's text, in which the conflict among affective perspectives can be made visible, indeed legible, to the philologist in him. The idea is that this conflict may thus be read symptomatically, but not only for its linguistic, historical, conceptual, or professional diagnosis. Rather, we are also to read this *"psychomachia,"* as the great contemporary Hans Ulrich Gumbrecht puts it, for what this conflict's "states or moods"—composing a material semiotics of the body—disclose about the conditions of life and the fate of the self, incarnated and played out as the modern subject of reading. This is because, as Klossowski, summarizing Nietzsche, puts it, "we [modern subjects] are only a series of discontinuous states in relation to the code of everyday signs ... about which the fixity of language deceives us."²

Nietzsche traces back (genealogically and physiologically) the concepts and ideas he is inscribing in his notebook to the contest of affects and the mix of conventional and innovative names for them. The hermeneutic intention here is to discover, at least momentarily, the impulses underlying and informing the particular dominant state or mood and its phantasms. These impulses shape the contest of affects in the subject, and really each one is a drive to dominate all the others by imposing its passionate perspective on the psyche as a whole. Such self-reading of the psyche as a shifting balance of forces can disclose, via the sign language of the external and interior motions of the body, the different truths befalling (often sublimely) the divided modern subject, as such. Nietzsche is truly the philologist of the body and its semiotics of powerful physical energies and its "high tonality of the soul [*hohe Stummung*]" (Klossowski 60).

We as critical readers may in turn disrupt and short-circuit identification with the conventional linguistic code of everyday signs for similar radical purposes. In fact, such radical disruption is precisely what literature since Plato has been accused of doing, which is why it often has been submitted to restrictive professional treatment. The long, slow eclipse of the paternal metaphor as the linchpin of psyche structure—I mix my metaphors advisedly here—suggests that reading, much as Auerbach on *Don Quixote* foretells, can lead to powerful dislocations, revolutions, and even mass psychosis. What Klossowski sees Nietzsche doing in his work is systematically and progressively, over the course of his career, detaching his ego, which Nietzsche often terms "Herr Nietzsche," from his consciousness (Klossowski 208–53). A consciousness without an ego is also a consciousness without a super-ego, as Klossowski notes, a thin membrane stretched tight as a defensive surface over the id, the abyss of the primary processes, which may inscribe their drives on its transparent inside, like an alien monster writing its messages to us from the other side of some quantum mirror.

In other words, Klossowski reads Nietzsche's final collapse into outright madness, whatever its physiological pathology, as the logical conclusion of a lifetime of self-experimentation in the disruption of the Nietzschean social identity ("Herr Nietzsche"). What stands clear in Nietzsche after this disruption, according to Klossowski, is an impersonal consciousness of raw psychic energies. These cosmic and quantum powers can then make use of the more impersonal medium of consciousness to learn to read for themselves. In this basic, albeit figurative, way, the forces and energies can then, through perspectival aphorism, speak and teach the truth inhering in such powers; that is, they can tell us what we are as modern embodied subjects of reading. Why is this significant? With these powers at our disposal, we may thus be able to begin to shape the future of humanity as a species, and on a planetary scale, in way which is more, not less, humane. We can thusly do battle against the monstrous seductions of the post-human imagination. For Klossowski, Nietzsche is, in this rather wildly idiosyncratic and often exuberantly self-parodying but all very human manner, the philologist of the future. The hermeneutic Übermensch may be *super*-human, but he is not *post*-human.

Despite the grand prospects of the title, *Visions of Global America and the Future of Critical Reading* has in fact a more modest, and mediated, goal and proceeds differently in terms of method and topic. In the subsequent chapters I am not so much interested in performing my own impersonalizing (or self-aggrandizing) *psychomachia*, à la

Klossowski's affective interpretation of Nietzsche, as I am in interpreting the formation of such an imperial subject of self-reading as a topic. In this sense, the emergence of the American empire stands as the sublime figure par excellence for the imaginative representational space in modernity within which such sublime self-creation primarily takes place.

"Global America," in other words, is the catachresis for what otherwise has no conventional name; it is a figure of speech. I use it to characterize the truth of the present and foreseeable moment in history of the modern culture of representation, by which I mean the conventional, and latest, forms of the mediation of information, knowledge, opinion, and their accompanying imaginaries. As we will see later in this book, this culture of representation is a system, and like all systems of countable elements, as Kurt Gödel demonstrated, it can be neither complete without self-contradiction nor coherent without being incomplete. The consequent necessary gap in the system of representation, which Alain Badiou terms the "null set" or "void," is the place where old imaginaries reemerge and new ones fleetingly manifest themselves—and just sometimes take hold in revolutionary ways. The luminous void (or "real" as Lacan would call it) is the limit site in the system of representation. It is subtracted from the system and signaled by self-evident contradiction and critical incompleteness. The void, in essence, opens onto the truth of the contemporary subject, which is this: it has become so plastic that it can transform into anything. Humanity is now becoming materially and physically the only species that is a non-species, for better and for worse. The technological and medical advances, from human genome mapping to cosmetic interventions, stand at the horizon of the present and the future that this book presumes, even as it focuses on the resources of the humanities, and especially literature, for meeting the challenge of the future of humanity in this context of a global and post-human America.

Part 1 of this book, "The Critical Apparatus," then presents in three interrelated chapters on Alain Badiou's eventful and subtractive theory of the subject of truth in the contexts of three contemporary global phenomena: fundamentalism, terrorism, and the role of the public intellectual. An intellectual of the present day, I contend, must be militantly critical in attempting to universalize new standards of truth and value in the emerging culture of the post-human imagination. This part thus presents the fullest version of my admittedly complex critical framework as it engages difficult contemporary contexts and considers how they bear on the future of humanity.

To put Badiou's insight in terms of the opening example from Auerbach: the truth event of Auerbach's reading is not so much his insight into the text of *Don Quixote* itself, nor is it the sacrifice of this insight he must make to the rigors of his professional method; rather, the truth event is this self-division in the modern reading subject itself. Auerbach can do nothing with this split but recognize it as he performs it, because he lacks a developed theory of the practice of reading. Such a theory must necessarily go beyond even the great diagnostic power of Paul de Man's "blindness and insight" allegories of reading; this is possible by adapting for reading what Badiou calls "truth-procedures." Badiou outlines these procedures most concretely in his study of St. Paul and the foundation of universalism, which I explore and develop in chapter 3.

By "truth procedures," I refer to the modes of fidelity to the fleeting and fugitive truth event that are available to the critical reader. The reader can use these modes to attempt to universalize its new truth into the present situation in which we find ourselves, thereby transforming current knowledge in potentially radical, if not revolutionary, ways. What I hope to do in this book, especially in its concluding chapter, is to begin to provide such a theory fully at work with such necessary accompanying procedures: Badiou's vision of the modern subject of truth and Lacan's theory of *le sinthome*. While all the chapters assume this Lacanian perspective, the specifics of the Joycean elements of the model of *le sinthome* are explored most fully in relationship to the work of James Purdy in chapter 9, "Bringing Out the Terror: James Purdy and the Culture of Vision."

Part 2, "The Literary Culture of Global America," beginning with chapter 4, "Global America and the Logics of Vision," explicates the two opposing logics of the visionary experience in American literature. Stemming from Ralph Waldo Emerson and Henry James, these competing logics have both confronted and interpenetrated one another for the last century and a half. Chapter 5, "America, the Symptom," clarifies this confrontation in light of my discussions on

Badiou's truth and Lacan's symptom and the real. I suggest that Emerson's and James's logics of vision haunt contemporary American Literature Studies, and in chapter 6, "Our Worldly Apocalypse," I illustrate how they both worked together in the mid to late 1970s to form what I call "the liberal decadence."

This is the period of the Carter administration, between the fall of the "Imperial Presidency" of Richard Nixon and the regressive de-sublimation of a genial primal (grandfather) mask, as worn by a truly ruthless Ronald Reagan. The moment in recent cultural history is in many ways a "time out of mind," as Bob Dylan might say, in which the established formations of the culture of representation are reestablished and new formations of its latest avatar, that of global America per se, were suspensefully suspended. A rare time of creative decadence in every sense and by every measure, this historical moment was also the time of maximum freedom for minorities, ethnics, and the marginalized of all sorts who, previously exiled at the edge of representation, were then offered the opportunity to perceive, to understand, and most of all, to move out and up.

Part 3, "The Exalted States of Reading," rediscovers and creatively repeats the high tonality of the antinomian and anarchic spirit of this lost time. These chapters focus on the presentation and performance, in the texts selected, of what Nietzsche characterizes as the highest tonality of the spirit, and what James—as I claim in chapter 7—calls "monstrous levity." This affect is a special sort of jouissance, as Lacan would say; Nietzsche calls it *"Stimmung,"* and it is best evoked in the following section (#337) of *The Gay Science*, which I will analyze in concluding this introduction:

> *The humanity of the future.*—When I view this age with the eyes of a distant age, I can find nothing odder in present-day man than his peculiar virtue of disease called 'the sense of history.' This is the beginning of something completely new and strange in history: if one gave this seed a few more centuries and more, it might ultimately become a wonderful growth with an equally wonderful smell that could make our old earth more agreeable to inhabit. We present-day humans are just beginning to form the chain of a very powerful future feeling [*Stimmung*], link by link—we hardly knew what we

are doing. It seems to us almost as if we are delaying not with a new feeling [*Stimmung*] but with a decrease in all old feelings [*Gefühlen*]: the sense of history is still something so poor and cold, and any are struck by it as by a frost and made even poorer and colder by it. To others it appears as the sign of old age creeping up, and they see our planet as a melancholy sick man who chronicles his youth in order to forget his present condition. Indeed, that is one color of this new feeling [*Gefühl*]: he who is able to feel the history of man altogether as his own history feels in a monstrous generalization all the grief of his youth, thinking of health, of the old man thinking of the dreams of his youth, of the lover robbed of his beloved, of the martyr whose ideal is perishing, of the hero on the eve after a battle that decided nothing but brought him wounds and the loss of a friend. But to bear and to be able to bear this monstrous sum of all kinds of grief and still be the hero who, on the second day of battle, greets dawn and his fortune as a person whose horizon stretches millennia before and behind him, as the dutiful heir to all the nobility of the past spirit, as the most aristocratic of old nobles and at the same time the first of a new nobility the likes of which no age has ever seen or dreamt: to take upon one's soul—the oldest, newest, losses, hopes, conquests, victories of humanity. To finally take all this in one soul and compress it into one feeling [*Stimmung*]—this would surely have to produce happiness unknown to humanity so far: a divine happiness full of power and love, full of tears and laughter, a happiness which, like the sun in the evening, continually draws on its inexhaustible riches, giving them away and pouring them into the sea, a happiness which, like the evening sun, feels richest when even the poorest fisherman is rowing with a golden oar! This divine feeling [*Stimmung*] would then be called—humanity![3] (190–91)

This valetudinarian, prophetic, and indeed ironically posthumous vision of the future of humanity celebrates the most sublime feeling—a mega-state or mood in sharp opposition to the dominant hegemony—and marks nothing less than a new nobility. Referred to in this translation simply as "humanity," the word *humanness* would capture more of Nietzsche's sense. This highest feeling, then, of humanness is a knot of metaphorical drives, which in their conceptual form Nietzsche calls doctrines: the eternal recurrence of the same, the will-to-power, and the overman.[4] Unlike what we might expect, the Übermenschen is all-too-humanly human.

As Klossowski makes clear, each above phrase of Nietzsche's visionary song to the future of humanity seemingly comes from the future itself, when Nietzsche will be long dead and living again in that age's over-human yet still human readers. Each phrase is a string of impulses, drives, and affects at work, each contesting with the other for dominance and self-definition, culminating with the transfiguration into an ideal, glorifying passion. The concept or idea of such a transformation represents, however, only a pale imitation of original raw impulses. This passage presents, in fact, a parody of the human ideal.

In addition, the passage embodies in its vision Nietzsche's three central doctrines in their most sublime form. Nietzsche would replace the personal unconscious of potentially creative people with the internalization of these doctrines as lived experiences. Foucault, I argue in chapter 8, "Toward a Global Democracy," follows Nietzsche's lead here (as does James Baldwin), by using a cosmic vision of sublimity to eradicate our given unconscious and replace it with a new, more humane one. James Purdy, as I argue in the next chapter, "Bringing Out the Terror," carries through the logic of this project with a vengeance. The eternal recurrence of the same, as we see from the above passage, is thus not some loony cosmological vision. Rather, it is a vision in which a newly emerging humanity, imaginatively superior to the humanity of Nietzsche's time and to all of the past, will assume upon itself via its greater historical sense all the affective experiences of the human past. Further, it will compress those feelings into its own super-feeling as described therein, and then release that feeling upon the world the way the sun in the evening transfigures all the world as it sets. The eternal return of the same is a repetition in a finer tone of the affective past of the species in the strength of the Nietzschean interpreter's aesthetic imagination. The squandering of energy of this transcendent mediating process is really the will-to-power in its most sublime form. So, too, the most effective of Nietzschean interpreters would be the preparatory human beings whose works prophesize the coming of the overman in this manner.

We can see Emerson, in the following excerpt from his *Journals*, approach his own distinctively American version of this Nietzschean vision:

> Perhaps after many sad, doubting, idle days, days of happy, honest labor will at last come when a man shall have filled up all the hours from sun to sun with great and equal action, shall lose sight of this sharp individuality which contrasts now so oddly with nature, and ceasing to regard, shall cease to feel his boundaries, but shall be interfused by nature and shall [so] interfuse nature that the sun shall rise by his will as much as his own hand or foot do now; and his eyes or ears or fingers shall not seem to him the property of a more private will than the sea and the stars, and he shall feel the meaning of the growing tree and the evaporating waters with a more entire and satisfactory intelligence than now attends the activity of his organs of sense. (*Journals*, V, 462–63)[5]

The major differences between Emerson's apocalypse and Nietzsche's is that Emerson's transcendent event occurs to the individual, while Nietzsche's is made to happen, as an event, to all *by* the super-individual who, like the sun, bestows transfiguring creativity like a gift. What's missing in Emerson is outgoing love; what is present in Nietzsche is just such love. This raises the question of whether Emerson is more honest than the dean of the school of critical suspicion. Or is Nietzsche, even Nietzsche, more loving (and lovable) than Emerson?

Of course, critics whose commitments are to a politics of identity could argue that both visions are compromised fatally by belonging to white, Euro-American, straight, privileged men. They would be right about everything, except the charge that being who and what they inevitably are fatally compromises these visions equally alike. The point I would make in distinguishing Nietzsche's active Whitmanian vision from Emerson's more passive spectral one (Whitman's self-identifications with the sun and Emerson's with snowy puddles are so strong they haunt even Wallace Steven's poetry) is that in becoming like the sun in the evening, one is becoming an enormous, impersonal, spontaneous "quantum" of discharging energy that, for better or worse (and most often for the better), transfigures the planet. Its existence is not only possible but also necessarily, beautifully justified. If one has to expend oneself totally in the end, I prefer this golden way to go. It gives joy (perhaps even jouissance) to oneself, in contrast to the grayer, chillier tones of Emerson's self-regard.

In any event, it is the argument of this book that this American difference, however we finally read and critically judge it, distinguishes global American culture. As I show in the concluding chapter, Henry James, the most cosmopolitan of our authors, puts these two essentially romantic visions and their wills-to-power into play most dramatically. As such, James's more inclusive, worldly vision would contest the ground and influence of the Emersonian dream of such perfected natural self-love that the Sage of Concord christened "self-reliance." Global America as the monstrous planetary automaton of *amour proper* versus any citizen of the world's spontaneous aesthetic transfiguration of the earth—this is the contest which *Visions of Global America and the Future of Critical Reading* enters on the side of what Nietzsche presents as "the future of humanity."

I CANNOT CONCLUDE this introduction without noting, for Americanists, that what follows is a visionary polemic. It draws sharp lines between the Emersonian and Jamesian traditions in American literature and culture. I do so because I have been reminded by important New Americanist scholars, such as Jonathan Arac and Donald E. Pease, that the Emerson and Emersonianism critiqued in these pages are but one strain, perhaps not the major one, in Emerson's own work. However that may be, I would argue, and do so herein, that what later generations take from Emerson is indeed essentially what I characterize in this book negatively. It may be that Emerson has brought many a simmering pot to boil, but if so he has done it while also punching holes in them. Similarly, as recent scholars, such as Wai Chee Dimock in *Through Other Continents: American Literature Across Deep Time* (Princeton University Press, 2006), have suggested, a globalized critical approach to American literature can defuse its imperial tendencies, making it but one among many literatures seen in their generic dimensions. In fact, such an approach, it seems to me, reinstates the homogenizing drive of culture under a liberal, multicultural smile. The key in this case is that all of the singular specificity of the languages of the various literatures, including that of American literature, is lost when a mishmash of snippets from the texts cited are rendered via the latest, albeit approved, translations and editions. In short, mine (like Slavoj Žižek's *In Defense of Lost Causes* [2008]) is an antithetical, contrarian book, but unlike the former's polemic, this one is more modest, critiquing contemporary literary and cultural studies in the name of the future of critical reading, not in that of global revolution. Of course, my belief is that unless we can read critically, such a revolution will never come.

Part One

THE CRITICAL APPARATUS

1

BADIOU'S TRUTH
AND THE OFFICE OF THE CRITIC

Neither Gods nor Monsters

WHEN I BEGAN reading science fiction at the height of the Cold War in the early 1960s, I became fascinated with the stories of a writer with the unlikely pen name of Cordwainer Smith. Paul M. A. Linebarger, the real name of the writer of these fantastic tales of the future, was a professor of what was then called Asiatic studies at the Johns Hopkins University, an expert in psychological warfare, and a civilian consultant to Army Intelligence.[1]

Smith's stories typically envision a future world, spanning many thousands of years, in which the Lords and Ladies of the Instrumentality, supported by supercomputers and other marvelous machines, supervise the production and distribution of "stroon," a drug synthesized from gigantic mutant sheep whose hides have become infected by an alien virus on a world called Norstrilia. Stroon grants near immortality in a time when other powerful drugs, incredible medical advances, and super prosthetic devices make a long life of a millennium or so not just possible but desirable.

This world is supported in various ways by the slave labor of robots and the Underpeople, a race of genetically engineered humanoid creatures derived from animal stocks. (There are also many different kinds of genetically altered human beings who have to perform specialized functions in the hostile environments of intergalactic space.) But it is the political and personal intrigues between the Underpeople and the Instrumentality that provide Smith's world with its greatest dramatic interest. These intrigues grow more complex and intense, even revolutionary, as telepathy and clairvoyance become increasingly widespread, first by mutation and then due to the selective (and clandestine) interventions in breeding practices made by the rebel Underpeople, another mysterious race of godlike aliens, and key enlightened members of the Instrumentality itself.

I have recalled this sci-fi world from the mists of my youth not for nostalgia's sake but because in many ways Smith's world, chronicled in his published work between 1950 and his untimely death (at age 53) in 1966, could virtually be the model of the world several recent books claim is emerging triumphantly or ominously (or both) right now.[2] In the following argument, I focus on one of these books, Elaine L. Graham's *Representations of the Post/Human: Monsters, Aliens and Others in Popular Culture,* because it is the most comprehensively informative and representative of them and, I think, highly instructive concerning typical critical attitudes toward what it attempts to define and then deploy as "the post/human."[3] At the end of this chapter, I will return to a discussion of why I think Smith's world does uncannily anticipate what has been called "our posthuman future."[4]

But before turning to that discussion, another introductory remark is in order. My subtitle, "Neither Gods nor Monsters," is derived (by double negation) from the toast that the evil old Dr. Pretorious makes to young Frankenstein in James Whale's classic 1935 horror film *The Bride of Frankenstein:* "To a new world of gods and monsters!" *Gods and Monsters* was also the title of the dramatized film biography of Whale released in 1999, which starred Ian McKellen. And it is, too, the title of Graham's concluding chapter about this cinematic toast (221). As the subtitle of this chapter may suggest, my ironic Nietzschean perspective would cast critical suspicion on all such hyperbolic imaginary speculations, a suspicion that this (like any) new world will remain in the end for most people "human, all too human."

The latest revolutions in biotechnology (largely associated in the popular mind with the Human Genome Project), in brain research and psychopharmacology, as well as those in digital technologies, have given rise to a variety of subcultures. Each of these has its own "worldview," and almost all of these worldviews deploy in their discourses some form of the term *post/human*. The one meaning that the different uses of this term generally share is an opposition to what is characterized as "modernity," which is portrayed in the discourses of these subcultures that are vying for hegemonic status in the new age as the culture of already empowered white male subjects who are up to no good: out to dominate nature, marginalize further so-called minority groups (however defined), and assume godlike status at the expense of all these "monstrous" others. That is, all these others have been "constructed" as monstrous in some fashion by being represented, classified, subjected, supervised, and disciplined (by modern culture) solely in order to determine by contrast a purified (albeit fictionalized) standard of (white male) normality. Although Graham's book contains a seventeen-page post/human bibliography in very tiny print, clearly the influence of only a few theorists shines through her basically feminist critical formulation of modernity. Among the most prominent and formative of these theorists for Graham's argument are Michel Foucault, Donna Haraway, and Bruno Latour. I focus on Graham's representative use of Foucault because he provides the announced critical framework and method. Regarding Haraway, more will follow from Graham herself.

Broadly speaking, then, the discourses of the post/human (for Graham), as they accompany developments in contemporary "technoscience," are generally oppositional discourses critical of current conceptions and realities of Western culture in many, often potentially conflicting, perhaps even self-contradictory, ways. This last is especially the case with technocratic futurists, who are critical of the status quo in contemporary society but in the name of their own desired white male hegemony. However that may be, my primary concern is not with the internal logic (or illogic) of these discourses; rather, my primary concern arises from two interrelated issues: the alleged affinity of their antihumanistic polemics with poststructuralism in general and Foucault specifically and the unrecognized nihilistic attitude they perpetuate. In a real sense, the centrality of Graham's book in this context is a testament to the fact that it has done its job admirably well: it does indeed effectively survey and taxonomically place the discourses of the post/human, and it does so better (more critically) than other recent texts. However, in its deployment of what Graham characterizes as a Foucauldian critical framework (and the avowed method of critical genealogies) and in the incomplete analysis of its own invocations of a Heideggerian perspective on modernity and technology, *Representations of the Post/Human,* already an excellent introduction to the topic, remains seemingly paralyzed on the threshold of the very comprehensive critique it apparently aspires to mount.

Before turning to the specifics of my critique of her representative work, however, I first need to give the reader at least some sketch of Heidegger's treatment of modernity and technology, since his vision of these phenomena helps define my own critical framework and represents, I believe, the fundamental step still not taken by Graham. The essence of modern technology, in fact of modernity per se, is what Heidegger calls in his various readings of Nietzsche "the will-to-will."[5]

This will-to-will, the reader will recall, is the underlying form of what Nietzsche could only see more metaphysically (in Heidegger's readings) as a universal and transhistorical "will-to-power." All forms of being—atoms, ants, and anthropoids—display, according to Nietzsche, a drive for ever-more power. Whatever quantum of power is observed and taken as a base state in relation to a configuration of other quanta of power, the entity under analysis will be seen as acting to secure an increasingly larger quantum of power, initially at least despite the consequences for itself or other entities. "Intelligence" in this context is basically an administrative phenomenon for directing the will-to-power in ways that, while still maximizing power, can avoid or at least postpone for as long as possible the worst consequences of its own fundamental drive. Why such postponement? In the case of living organisms, so that reproduction may occur, and a potentially infinite future be made possible for the entity in question.

What Heidegger proposes in his readings of Nietzsche's will-to-power is that modernity's form of this will is more precisely depicted as the-will-to-will: that is, as a will to itself in an infinite circuit of becoming through all the modes of being. It is a process of self-revision both captured in the staged spectacles of the modern will's self-images and housed in modernity's various media archives. In this severe light, the modern subject can be seen as nothing more than an endlessly self-revising and self-recording performance artist with shocking masks, some drawn from the archives of the past, some from the imagination (perhaps now, the post/human imagination) of the future. That these masks may be made of reanimated dead flesh, silicon chips, and animal fur, or that they may penetrate the skin and serve as invasive prosthetic devices, matters little, analytically speaking. "Humanist," "antihumanist," or "posthumanist," all modes of existence in modernity are manifestations of this nihilistic will-to-will. For Heidegger, this modern condition is a historical epoch of potentially millennial expanse.

But why is it nihilistic? After all, nihilism means that existence is seen as valueless, and certainly the discourses of modernity and of the post/human are awash in a sea of values, of value assertions, of value designations, of the conflict of values, and so on. For Heidegger, following Nietzsche, once it is shown that the highest values of the Judeo-Christian tradition have devalued themselves, the production of new values is then a project always strangling itself in its own crib, as it were. How can this be?

The highest value of the Judeo-Christian tradition is truth, according to Nietzsche and Heidegger. This tradition's God is the true one, and this God demands truth from all believers: truth in speaking to and loving others and truth in praying and confessing to this God. For the better part of two thousand years, this tradition bred human subjects to be seekers of the truth. With the emergence of modern science, the quintessential method for seeking truth, the Judeo-Christian tradition bred its own executioner. Not only has modern science discovered the falsity at the basis of this tradition, but it has led to the prospect that there are only lies, only appearances, only untruths. All truths, and so all "true" values, are necessary fabrications useful in the will-to-power's (or the will-to-will's) quest to secure ever more power long enough to pass on such accumulated power to posterity. To what end? No end, only the ever-enhanced prospect of this endless process of self-revising will-to-will itself. (Heidegger stresses repeatedly that the value of imaginary or real self-enhancement, at the expense of all else, is the nihilistic "value" par excellence.) In this nihilistic context Heidegger concludes that not only Nietzsche's philosophy but any philosophy can at best now do nothing, for otherwise it will participate in and help to perpetuate such apparently endless nihilistic self-enhancement:

> Philosophy will be unable to effect any immediate change in the current state of the world. This is true not only of philosophy but of all purely human reflection and endeavor. Only a god can save us. The only possibility available to us is that by thinking and poetizing we prepare a readiness for the appearance of a god . . . insofar as in view of the absent god we are in a state of decline. (Graham 224)

It is interesting to note that the verb *to enhance* and its nominal variants appear in Graham's book too many times to count, virtually every couple of pages or so.

Admittedly, such a seemingly quietist response of Heidegger's, attempting to think and to poetize only so as to prepare a readiness for a god's appearance, does not appeal to the habitual activist impulses of the vast majority of modern intellectuals. What does appeal nowadays, of course, is representing one's critical efforts as being part of a large struggle against the powers that be, a struggle for greater justice, that is, a struggle for greater access to and distribution of the material and cultural resources of modernity, for all people, and now including, in light of the post/human imagination, all possible beings. Each and every subject, in this best of all possible worlds that is emerging, should form itself on the model of the nihilistic will-to-will according to the ultimate "value" of a potentially infinite self-enhancement that can recognize no limits to the course of its sensational transgressions.

This is where a certain reading of Foucault comes into play in most other varieties of contemporary oppositional discourse, post/human or otherwise. This reading of Foucault ignores or downplays the problematic of nihilism that Foucault inherits from Nietzsche and Heidegger, despite his repeated invocations of this inheritance in his interviews and writings. This informed ignorance, as I like to think of it, derives from the opportunism of reading Foucault as making possible a positive conception of critical agency to effect substantial change in ways Foucault would never countenance. What, more specifically, then, is this reading? It is a reading that presents Foucault as a social constructionist and new historicist critic of modernity's institutions and discourses who is supportive of a liberal or socially democratic vision of all kinds of self-revising subjectivities.[6] Well, you might say, isn't this Foucault? I do not think it is, and I have argued for a different darker vision of Foucault, a Foucault given to radical parodies of each and every one of the ever-emerging discourses of modernity.[7] My "Foucault," as it were, is a knowing instance of the Nietzschean will-to-power or the Heideggerian will-to-will. Foucault, in this sense, is preparing a readiness for thinking and poeticizing "beyond modernity" (or is it "behind its back"?) by playing out, via savage ironies, all the discursive possibilities of modernity, even those still in the process of emerging even now, such as the post/human. Like Nietzsche's Socrates in *The Twilight of the Idols,* Foucault wills his own death as a figure or idol, so as to take as many of the discourses of incipient nihilism as possible with him into the black hole of his radical parodies. Unfortunately, again like the dying Socrates, Foucault has been taken with full seriousness, when he would have preferred to have inspired demonic laughter instead.

But isn't such laughter a testament to nihilism, too? Of course, for right now (however long that is), there simply is no escape from nihilism. This does not mean that we should all fall on our swords. What is does mean, however, is that we should all stop and try to think. Thinking in modernity is not an easy task to perform. As Paul A. Bové has demonstrated over the last decade or so in his many essays on various aspects of Henry Adams and his work, thinking is perhaps the most important thing we can do and the thing we are least prepared to do by modernity. In this respect, at least, I think Nietzsche, and Heidegger, certainly would have concurred with Bové's Adams.[8]

So, for purposes of argument, let us agree that attempting to think and to poeticize a readiness for a form of being beyond an endlessly self-revising and nihilistic modernity is an experiment that, whether itself nihilistic or not in the final analysis, generally has not been tried in sustained ways by modern intellectuals and especially not by contemporary academic critics. Why not? I think it is because such attempts could possibly lead to where Heidegger's did, to a contemplation of what he calls, in the previously cited passage, "the absent god," who is neither quite the gone god nor quite a here one, either. Such an absent god is clearly a stand-in for the mode of temporality we call the future, and it is in this mode of the future per se that this absent god paradoxically embodies best, by its very formative absence, the nonhuman dimension of existence. I say "nonhuman" deliberately to distinguish, terminologically at first, what I am indicating as being different from the human or the post/human or, for that matter, the inhuman.[9]

What does my "nonhuman" dimension of existence refer to? And how is it related to the divine, the religious, or the sacred? Is it fundamentally different from the post/human? If so, in what way? Let me try to answer these questions by testifying to my own religious sensibility: I contain multitudes of conflicting fragments of modern subjectivities (or is it legions?).

I follow Jacques Derrida in his recent work in identifying the conflicted core of three of the world's great religions—Judaism, Christianity, and Islam—with the story of Abraham and Isaac.[10] This story, as read most imaginatively by Kierkegaard, defines for me my sense of the divine as the radically nonhuman. I will recall here only the basic outlines of the story.

Abraham has finally been given a son by his previously barren wife, Sarah, thanks to God's miraculous intervention. Now God commands that Abraham sacrifice this child. Abraham sets out to do just that, in strict obedience to God's divine command. Before he can execute this sacrifice, however, Gods sends an angel to intervene, and a ram is sacrificed instead of Isaac.

The mysterious inscrutability of both God and Abraham in this story is what perplexes and performs the sense of the radically nonhuman, or divine. It inspires an infinite anxiety in Kierkegaard, endless "fear and trembling." This story is a dramatic figuration of the impossible coming to pass, in each of its narrative moments and as a narrative whole. This impossibility is not just cognitive; it is also emotional. It is total, and it marks the limits of the human, surely, but also of the inhuman, which so readily, via the aesthetic concept of the sublime, can be subsumed into a consumable interpretation along the lines of "Ho-Hum, another mountain or abyss to imaginatively divine myself in." Similarly, the post/human, the next "demonic" phase in the human species, can be readily plotted into a historical trajectory (positive or negative, progress or decadence) that itself is humanly understandable, even if the post/human's initial manifestations may be a bit confusing or upsetting. Such master plotting, after all, is what Graham (deploying her Foucault) is doing in her representative text. But what "moral" does the story of Abraham and Isaac exemplify? Morals have been drafted for the story, of course, but what sort of God or father would produce or play along with such a story, if what the tale teaches is this: God demands blind obedience, Abraham alone gives it, and therefore Abraham and his disposable-in-principle descendants ironically become "a light to all nations," informing all the absurdly gratuitous cruelty and mysterious wisdom of this deity and his chosen one. This unique moral will surely pack the tents now, won't it?

No, I think this story, at the heart of Judaism, Christianity, and Islam, really stands for, performs, each time it is read and reflected critically on, the radically nonhuman, the divine, as the impossible that is ever to come and does indeed come, only in ways that we cannot recognize or understand, which is why we should be wary of any secular or religious invocations of human beings now becoming gods themselves, or even eagerly awaiting any such gods. Heidegger's impossibly "absent god," who nonetheless ironically makes possible the thinking and poeticizing of the impossible ever to come, is more than enough for me. Why? With this question in mind, I think we can now most usefully turn to *Representations of the Post/Human*.

Graham provides in her introduction a map of the post/human by establishing a polarity within which the discourses of the subcultures concerned with the topic can be placed, as on a spectrum or continuum. One pole she terms "technophobic," and this position sees the latest developments of science and their technological applications to society as forms of further "enslavement" (6) à la Aldous Huxley's *Brave New World* or George Orwell's *Nineteen Eighty-Four*. The other pole Graham designates "technophilic," and this position champions these latest developments as "liberation," even "salvation" (16) à la technocratic, even technopagan, celebrations of a pseudo-Nietzschean vision of the material realization of humanity's superhuman destiny. In between these poles, she places an assortment of discourses in an array of critical genealogies, based on their tendency to lean more toward one pole than another. These discourses, given critical genealogies by Graham, include classical myths about and commentary on monsters, science fiction classics (such as Mary Shelley's *Frankenstein*), hermetic speculations (ancient and Renaissance), utopian and dystopian visions, transhumanist polemics, technocratic futurism, cyberpunk fiction, feminist cyborg writing, popular cinema and television shows, and everything else conceivably dealing with the post/human. She conveniently defines the post/human as the radical intermixing of the human, the mechanical, and the so-called natural in its organic and inorganic physical forms. Even Jewish folktales about the golem, their sources and legacies in modern literature and film, find a place in her map of the post/human. Along the way, the reader also learns something about the traditional study of monsters, which is termed "teratology."

This tremendous synoptic range adds to the reader's sense that under Graham's capacious gaze the post/human as a category is fruitfully collecting many phenomena and providing them all with the same general name in a fashion useful to contemporary cultural criticism. By deploying as her critical framework a social constructivist and new historicist Foucault, she is able to debunk in whatever discourse she is interrogating any would-be essentialist pretensions and naturalistic assumptions almost before they raise their own ugly heads. But with this brand of Foucault, Graham can also keep reminding the reader that her own critical discourse is always only comparatively gathering and provisionally identifying, with as much of an account of the differences as possible; what it nonetheless is presenting is a postmodern sort of unity, namely, the post/human. However much I think her Foucault is incorrect, her strategic use of Foucault in this admittedly conventional fashion enables her to measure and judge, while avoiding, for the most part, committing any of the sins, essentialist or otherwise, she finds lurking in or rampaging through other discourses. In this fashion, Graham is very good at sweeping the sanctuary of the contemporary academy clean of most essentialist debris.

An exemplary case in point, and a difficult case (for feminist political reasons) for her to take on, appears in Graham's extended analysis of Donna Haraway's work. Graham discusses much of Haraway's feminist cultural criticism, from her famous 1985 essay, "A Cyborg Manifesto," to her 1997 book, *Modest Witness@Second Millennium. FemaleMan©_Meets_OncoMouse™: Feminism and Techno-*

science. As Graham summarizes Haraway's general position (taken from her 1992 book, *Primate Visions: Gender, Race, and Nature in the World of Modern Science*), "simians, cyborgs and women all occupy the boundaries of modernity, positioned there to show forth the scientific and cultural narratives that determine what will count as knowledge" (2003). One can, of course, slide into the slot under the rubric of "women" one's own preferred "monstrous minority," which is rather the point of both Haraway's original position and Graham's analytic use of it here.

Haraway is a feminist cultural critic of scientific modernity and a scientist herself. She not only argues her position announced above but attempts to perform it in her own writing, which she dubs "cyborg writing." Such writing would be, like poststructuralist *écriture*, both subversively disruptive of the binary logics of modernity in matters of race, class, gender, and species, *and* celebratory of the hybrid, permeable boundaries of cultural existence, because of the ever greater possibilities for human (and beyond human) subjectivities it now supposedly can foster. Cyborg writing is to conventional discourses what the cyborg is to the categories of humanity, nature, and technology recognized by the grand philosophical tradition; that is, such cyborg writing would make a vital mess of rigid demarcations. In this formulation, the blurring of class, race, gender, of life, death, human, and post/human, will ultimately promote the liberations of new possibilities of existence on the planet.

In characterizing Haraway's position and writing in this way, however, Graham does not intend to reduce Haraway to the belated legacy of a romantic modernism intersecting with critical theory's desperate hunger for "the next big thing." Haraway's is no simple-minded Rousseauistic vision for Graham. If there are any inheritances, they are Byronic in manner, mediated by Shelley's *Frankenstein*. As Graham remarks apropos of Haraway's figure of the cyborg and what it is intended to represent:

> Her cyborg has endured no fall from primordial innocence, no Oedipal crisis, but also has no need, equally, therefore of a narrative of restoration. Cyborgs [are without families of any kind, and so] do not crave holism or reunification with abandoned paradises nor maternal [or patriarchal] figures; instead, like Haraway's other favorites, the

tricksters, cyborgs are restless nomads . . . so Haraway's narrative of redemption is [then] about transition and change without loss, permanent wandering and transmutation without origins or ultimate destination. (206)

Whatever romantic analogies or paradigms for Haraway might be appropriate, Graham demonstrates that for this feminist cultural critic of modernity, neither narrative of progress nor visions of apocalypse are required. In fact, as Graham details for most of an entire chapter, the ultimate expression of the modern Western binary logic Haraway wants to disarticulate and surmount is precisely the religious logic that pits spiritual transcendence against material embodiment (213–18), and, certainly, this "progressive" critical position of Haraway's is indebted, broadly speaking, to a recognizably post-Cartesian romantic social and cultural project that has revolutionary dimensions.

As Graham underscores, Haraway was raised a Roman Catholic, which touts officially an incarnational and sacramental religious vision. One can generally find in her work that "her opposition between human and divine, or (technolog-ized) earth and (immaterial) heaven itself rests upon unexamined [binary] constructions of 'religion and transcendence' that owe their origins to the Western Enlightenment" (217) and also to what I take specifically to be its secularized Protestant and politically revolutionary discourses. Consequently, Graham concludes that while Haraway's cyborg writing demonstratively embraces "contingency and complicity [with irresolvable complexities], it can do so only in a mood predominantly suffused with irony," and thus it can only adopt "a postmodern veneer in its embrace of the hybridity and contingency of techno scientific culture" (218). In short, despite her most influential feminist cultural essay being entitled, after Foucault, "Situated Knowledges" (collected in *Primate Visions*), Haraway apparently is not the real thing—she's no Foucault (as Graham understands him), who did famously prophesize the so-called "death of man." In Graham's view, Haraway's cyborg writing permits the re-coalescence of the rigid binary structures of modern thinking that it would explode precisely because of its not fully examined and critiqued, post-Enlightenment religious underpinnings. In other words, Haraway is not enough of a social constructivist and new historicist critic, but is more of a powerfully diverting (albeit belatedly romantic) theoretical practitioner of modern irony.

I have discussed Graham's representative critique of Haraway at some length because it is so indicative of her avowedly Foucauldian critical framework and interpretive method, and because, from my admittedly untimely critical point of view, Graham misses the most important matter. She misses it specifically with regard to Haraway's would-be cyborg writing (whatever that is supposed to really mean and do) and more generally concerning all the talk of the post/human. What is that, you say? There is no post/human—yet! What Haraway says about the figure of the cyborg and the kind of writing she wants to write in its name is all imaginary. It has no material reality to it (yet) and perhaps never will. No monsters, mythic or otherwise, left us their thousand years of cultural history. Nor, as far as we know, have any godlike aliens dropped off their packets of instant worlds to mix up with a few of our spare tears. Nothing like that has popped into existence. And nothing of the Internet and its virtual realities has subverted anything in the real world of global capitalism; rather, all these developments have only enhanced the spread of capitalist power into every nook and cranny of existence, proliferating and accelerating the alienated and alienating work rhythms of our lives. There is no such thing as a vacation anymore; there are no holidays in reality for us; there is no respite from an increasingly driven will-to-will ever new value(s).

This is not to say that Graham's book is not an important or effective one. In fact, its organization is quite effective for the purposes of its argument. With its many mythic monsters, hermetic homunculi, Jewish golems, Frankenstein's monsters (original story and subsequent cinematic adaptations), cyberpunk terminators, the alien Borg (from the later *Star Trek* TV shows and films), the realities and dreams of artificial intelligence, and goddess "theology," her book repeatedly stages not a continuous history of the same idea so much as critical genealogies of the cultural sites and archeological spaces, where all sorts of questions—What is human? Who is human? Is it better to be more or less human, or better still to be a god? And then, what kind of divinity, a fully embodied technopagan god or an apocalyptically disembodied Cartesian ghost or a latter-day Protestant spirit in the machine body of a superplanetary computer?—can be shown to have appeared sequentially in the system of representation defining modern Western culture, now with a most irresistible planetary reach. What Graham's book thus demonstrates most importantly, I think, is that the post/human now defines the latest imaginative horizon within which the poststructuralist global intellectual can define an identity. The post/human is, in this context, not the only, but surely the most powerful (because most comprehensive), if clearly not the most logically coherent, game in town.

But what if a critic doesn't want to play this game of identities and identifications? What then? This question is not entirely my question. It is the question that I believe informs, silently, at least in some large part, this concluding paragraph of Graham's own book:

> In many respects, therefore, it is legitimate to regard the emergent cybernetic, biotechnological and digital age as representing a new era of post/human history. Yet in other ways, the contemporary West retains a marked degree of continuity with more ancient cultures that first dreamed of gods and monsters at the margins of human imagining. And exploration of the many different hopes and fears surrounding the impact of advanced technologies requires, as I have been arguing, a full register of representational practices, cultural, literary, mythical and scientific. Monsters, aliens and others still function as important monitors and mediators of understandings of what it means to be post/human, not least in the indeterminacy, their eschewal of ontological purity, and their attention to human nature as defined by boundaries rather than essences. They embody the disturbing reminders of difference at the heart of unitary identity, and they suggest that any post/human ethic can be neither an escape into technocratic invulnerability nor a retreat into the imaged purity of organic essentialism. Rather, as I have argued, it will be about the pleasures and risks of multiple allegiances, contingent identities and nomadic sensibilities. Fantastic encounters with representations of the post/human offer important insights into the many meanings of being human, but they are also devices by which new worlds can be imagined. (233–34)

I want to conclude this chapter, however, not by critically reflecting on Graham's self-evidently heartfelt but also half-hearted hesitations here in this concluding passage of her book, but by thinking about the larger questions of contemporary critical identity formation and its necessary relationship to the post/human.

What does it really matter in a truly impersonal way whether or not there is a "designer baby," cyborg writing, or a spaced-out virtual reality freak who may or may not have taken the required psychotropic medication today? What does it matter that the material and cultural resources of the emerging post/human imagination be more (rather than less) equally distributed? And if each one of us (or our professional group) is able to play out, on a brief break from our alienated labor, the fantasy of Dr. Frankenstein, so what? Once the last person or group on earth can become whatever she, he, or it wants to be, what then? That insatiable modern will-to-will indeed will—*must*—not rest, cannot rest, because its only aim is an impossible infinite self-enhancement. But what if the universe is as perfect as it can be already at every moment, and what if any change, however tiny, however carefully done, means everything existing is abolished as it is, and so all begins to swing wildly out of kilter, like those complex physical systems (such as our weather systems on the planet), wobbling ever more crazily toward an absolute chaos that the madly beautiful figures of fractal geometry enshrine? What then?

My point in raising such questions as these is not to suggest that I, or anyone, know the answers. Precisely the opposite is the case. No one can ever know the answers about the whole, because no one, however enhanced by modern technology, can ever know the whole, much less pretend to judge its value. No one can become the post/human god; the administrative imaginary of global capitalism is itself busy with the production of this god's simulacra, *especially* in the harshest discourses of its severest critics. This particular dimension of critical imagination as an unintended repetition of the very thing it would overcome is the consequence of existence in such an epoch of nihilism as ours. All such "developments" compose the lesson of the unknowable (delivered in part from critical reflections on quantum physics and its theories) that few wish to recall now in this moment of global capitalism's apparent ascendancy.[11] It is just such recollection of the unknowable when projected into an imaginary cultural future that Smith's science fiction stories repeatedly perform and so uncannily anticipate for us now, but here is not the place for a full discussion of his work.¹²

I do think it is appropriate, however, to conclude here by remarking that the post/human imagination, however romantic or modernist, produces largely prophetic discourses, like Smith's, but the post/human also produces discourses that, unlike those composing Smith's world, too often lose sight of their own fictional status as works of the imagination. In its rather desperate, not to say hectic, anticipation of "the next big thing" in modern cultural development, even if, or especially if, it should be modernity's transcendence by one or another "monstrous birth" of the post/human, this contemporary imagination forgets the sanguine history of the figure of monstrous births and its painful problematic in literary, cultural, and political discourses.¹³ (My own ironic critical performance here has been intended to preempt such cultural amnesia by provoking the reader to remember this legacy.)

Smith's world, in the end, decides to remember such figures and all their mortal problematics, and does so by intentionally rediscovering, as part of its imagined ultimate (and generally peaceful) revolution, the inveterately creaturely status of humanity—a humanity for whom all divine (or demonic) creators, eagerly invoked or scorned, are impossibly, joyfully absent:

> Oh, you will see, you will see
> Them striding fair, oh fair and free!
> Down garden paths of silver grass
> Past flowing rivers,
> Their hair pushed back
> By fingers of the wind.
>
> And you will know them
> By their blank white faces,
> Expressionless, removed,
> All lines smoothed,
> As they stride on in the night
> Toward their unimaginable goals . . . ¹⁴

And good riddance to all these deliberately absent-minded ones!¹⁵

NAMING THE MILITANT MULTIPLES OF THE VOID

When the poet uses the word *flower,* Stephan Mallarme famously declares, the flower that is missing from all the bouquets in the world appears in the text. The poet, that is, does not mirror a particular existing flower, nor does he express his personal ideal of flowery perfection. Rather, the poet impersonally invokes and summons to appearance the spectral flower subtracted from and haunting these conventional collections of flowers as fits within the terms of their arrangements. As such, this poetic flower is not some positive Platonic idea or paradigm of perfection but the signifying negation of all positive presentations, the militant void of multiple differences. Once so evoked, this subtracted specter or virtually indiscernible ghost of a flower then receives a new name from the poet via his innovative use of figures and speech. This simple formulation of a complex theory of truth as event and its relationship to being can stand as a rough guide to Alain Badiou's *Being and Event.*[16]

Potential critics might quarrel with Mallarme or Badiou about this apparently dialectical relationship of critique and negation between the already known structure of existing flowers and the poet's new imaginative flower. For however critical and negating it might be, the structure would condition, perhaps even determine, the poet's imagination. But both Mallarme and Badiou resist such slick logical tricks, because they embrace infinite multiplicity and radical contingency. The poet's virtual flower is by definition, then, not the recollected Platonic norm but the repeated occurrence of the unknown truth of monstrosity.

Badiou's theory of truth, in his newly translated masterwork, combines the major elements of the two competing conceptions of truth: truth as correspondence and truth as unveiling. These two theories have dominated the Western philosophical tradition since the ancient Greeks. Unlike Martin Heidegger (his major predecessor here), however, Badiou does not definitively subsume one conception of the truth to another, as a lesser or fallen derivation of the privileged conception. Heidegger argues, of course, that the correspondence model of truth derives from the unveiling model. The truth of a being must show itself to us before we can tell if any statement about this truth corresponds to it or not. (Of course, the internal coherence model of truth, that a statement is true if it coheres, is logically consistent, with the other statements of a system, has largely been compromised by Kurt Gödel's famous proof that shows no system can be both coherent and complete, for there is always an element in the system for which the terms of the system cannot rationally account.) However that may be, for Badiou, the event of truth emerges in the void or gap in every situation, the abyss that separates what the situation presents and what it represents. The truth of this void is in itself an indiscernible multiple that only retrospective and retroactive truth procedures begin to define.

The way the U.S. Constitution defines a nation that includes as *elements* (women, African Americans, Indians) what it originally fails to represent as *citizens* is a good example of what Badiou is getting at with his theory of truth as event and of truth procedures that flesh out and realize that event ex post facto. The event of truth introduces into the world a new, previously inconceivable universal that is then materialized piecemeal but never totally via truth procedures.

To understand better Badiou's theory of truth, which is clearly indebted to Gödel and Heidegger, as well as to Paul Cohen's 1963 innovations in set theory, requires for my purposes putting it in the context of both Jacques Lacan's and Michel Foucault's related yet fundamentally different conceptions. Lacan's formula for the subject's relationship to truth is by now familiar, and by repetition, perhaps, all too familiar. The subject receives the truth only via the other—and only in inverted and so misrecognized form. This is the truth of the unconscious, of the ineluctable signifying chain, and, in its extreme form, the truth of madness, psychosis. In other words, the noncorrespondence, in the mode of ironic opposition, between truth and the subject's statement of it constitutes Lacan's parodic analysis of truth as correspondence. This is, in short, truth as systematic noncorrespondence and nonrecognition. Naturally, the power of the analytic recognition of such nonrecognition and noncorrespondence, which the analysand, via the relationship to the analyst, may come to assume, is itself, however ironically theoretical, a form of recognition and correspondence. The problem of truth for Lacan is one that summons our most intense research into all the dimensions of the subject and its world, even if Lacan's primary focus in his career is analytic, on the truth or nontruth of interpretative signification, and not comprehensively affective, on the full range of the experience of truth, especially as his *Seminar on Anxiety* does offer much food for further thought to his disciples.

If Lacan provides Badiou with an ironic legacy concerning truth—truth is the noncorrespondence of the correspondence theory of truth—then Foucault, in his later work, discusses at considerable length the conditions of possibility—the historical, political, and rhetorical conditions—by which the subject may speak the truth, especially to power. *Parrhesia,* truth telling, for Foucault, is the central pivot around which the ancient subject's efforts of ethical self-stylization, what he calls the subject's relationship of truth, are highlighted in the erotic mode. This erotic mode is imagined as an eros that is increasingly sublimated into and internalized as a self-mastering quest for truth conducted by lover and beloved alike. No centralized state or church authority regulates such truth or its pursuit. The most important procedures, with Stoicism, are those involving the central relationship of the subject to the chosen master as that relationship gets incorporated into an elected style of life appropriate for oneself. Significantly, this relationship to the master is the gateway to the greater relationship to the sublime vision of the cosmos that the adept is meant to experience so that the Stoic wisdom may take all the better. The invention of a true subject, that is, a subject true to its self-chosen and self-styled second nature, is what Foucault means finally by truth. What Lacan postulates about the transformation of the subject's symptom into *le sinthome,* with James Joyce in *Finnegans Wake,* can be read as providing a psychoanalytic parallel to Foucault's vision of the true subject.

With both Lacan and Foucault, we see two aspects of truth: its fugitive self-opposing nature and its procedural setting. The Stoic practices of self and the psychoanalytic centrality of the clinic provide the procedural setting, whether institutionalized or improvised, within which the fugitive emergence of truth as the inverted correspondence and signification of the unconscious signifier and signified may occur.

Badiou thinks of truth as both the event and the procedures of fidelity to that event which the subject, inaugurated by that event, produces. In this view, the subject is not conceived as a person or even a position. Rather, it is thought of as "any local configuration of a generic procedure from which a truth is supported" (391). In other words, the subject functions as a formal space, and, as such, it maybe locally inhabited by a person, a couple, a group, or even, rarely, a people. Truth procedures, however, are generic or universal, "global" in our terms: they are the rationally accessible rules for the initiation, transmission, and verification of the subject within the truth of the situation so far as it continues to exist, however un- (or under-) recognized it may be. The absent "flowers" of art, revolution, scientific discovery, or eros receive new names, which, as an ethical imperative, always must be seen as containing elements that cannot be nailed down, filled out, realized, or made more substantial. The event of truth and the procedures of naming enable us to perceive at the edge of the void the repeated emergence of these unnamable militant multiples of situation after situation, until all are free.

Within any situation, the elements of that situation are established as its members by a count or inventory, which establishes the state of the situation, and we should take "state" here in all its senses. Since being, for Badiou, is the inchoate prospect of infinite multiples without end, human beings construct a situation out of such a prospect in piecemeal fashion, using much smaller portions of that prospect and establishing order within them by means of the count. The principle of selection of any count determines what elements of the situation remain presented elements and what become representative members.

Badiou's point is true for all aspects of the situation, but because every count or inventory of the situation also necessarily involves the terms for representing that count or inventory, the count or inventory always produces more terms as members of the situation than there are elements originally presented, even as certain elements are not represented by the count or inventory. To put it in structural terms, the State structure of any situation always excludes and includes more than it could or should. There is always a gap or void between the presented and represented situation.

Without getting into Badiou's explanatory mathemes and uses of set theory here, we can say that for him there are always more elements presented by a situation than get represented in it by the count and its structures of definition and determination, and the production of terms used to represent the members of the situation always result in more empty figures than ones with determinate referents. This superfluity or overdetermination of terms, arising from the indetermination or destitution of elements, is Badiou's application of the concept of the null set from set theory to the situation of truth per se. Rightly or wrongly, I read Badiou's resorting to mathematics as his composing his dark conceit of ontology, his allegory of being, from a once traditional but now unconventional discipline, for the sanctioned novelty's sake. It would be as if a critic resorted to the lineaments of Spenserian allegory to discuss the vision of modernism. The reductive vision of "Being" in the title of his book serves to make possible Badiou's conception of truth as event.

A subject comes into existence, then, when the event of truth forces the use of terms, of names, whose referent is not in the situation as represented but may be a repressed or simply missing element of it. Badiou calls this feature "a hole in knowledge" (431). Such "a hole in knowledge" is the void or real of any situation, in Lacan's terms. It is what in large part makes the event of truth and its consequences radically contingent and unforeseen, indeed unforeseeable. Such terms or names can gain their referents, Badiou contends, only after the fact—they will have been true when the event of truth that inaugurated the critical intervention of this novel usage of language has been more fully realized in the situation, which is at the moment only just emerging. *The subject and its relationship to truth in Badiou turn out always to have been prophetic, even as the new situation that the improvised imagination of available terms conjures up must appear to be utopian at first:*

> [Unlike the terms of an ideology], the names used by the subject—who supports the local configuration of a generic truth—*do not, in general, have a referent in the situation.* Therefore, they do not double the established language. But then what use are they? These are words which do not designate terms, but terms which "will have been" presented in a *new* situation: the one which results from the addition to the situation of a truth (an indiscernible) of that situation. With the resources of the situation, with its multiples, its language, the subject generates names whose referent is in the future anterior: this is what supports belief. Such names "will have been" assigned a referent, or a signification, when the situation will have appeared in

which the indiscernible—which is only [figuratively] represented (or included)—is finally presented as a truth of the first situation. . . . Every subject can thus be recognized by the emergence of a language which is internal to the situation but whose referent—multiples are *subject to the condition* of an as yet incomplete generic part that is yet to come [in the emerging new situation]. (398, original italics)

These names and terms are not snatched out of the air, of course, but are present in the situation, yet not represented there, thanks to the state of the count. These new names are subtracted from the count, kept out of it, and deployed as both critique of the situation and prophecy of the situation to come. They are then submitted to a radical process of more precise and more specific *indetermination* by the selective and scrupulous use of irony, ambiguity, paradox, catachresis—in short, by the rigorous operation of imaginative figuration. Badiou's own use of mathematics may be seen as a rather novel version of such figuration operating on the state of the situation in poststructuralist philosophy. Such terms, in any event, are thereby *subtracted* from, and so institute that original hole in, knowledge. Such poetic use of terms thus is put into play as the figures of the truth to come (432), to which the truth procedures we establish would maintain fidelity.

To my mind, then, Badiou, in *Being and Event,* whatever all his announced intentions, is clearly providing us with a poetics of truth, and perhaps *the* poetics of truth we have needed for reading and analyzing literature with a more sensitive perception than recently seen in literary studies.

Thus, we can say following Badiou that a situation contains elements which are counted as members in order to structure and secure the state of that situation, as such. The institution that performs this representative inventory is most often the State in the largest sense, but can be seen as any administrative agency from that of the ego on up. In making this count, the State neglects to represent elements in the situation that are determined as not fitting due to perceived or asserted contradiction, even as the State also ironically produces many more representative but essentially empty terms for the situation. The event of truth is a contingent discovery of the subject of the situation, who then must use the indeterminate terms figuratively and with precision, and can do so thanks to irony, ambiguity, paradox, and all the other resources of figuration. These newly appropriated terms can acquire their referents only from the perspective of the new situation as it emerges and completes itself according to the logic and direction of the truth procedures established by (and establishing) the subject of the emerging situation. Although not presented in *Being and Event,* Badiou's major example is the case of Saint Paul. I will address Badiou's treatment of Paul in detail in the next two chapters, but his position must be briefly sketched out here.

In conclusion, Badiou argues apropos Saint Paul that the event of truth that struck him down on the Road to Damascus was that of the Resurrection, that faith in that truth superseded all the rituals of the law, even the law itself, and that the sole truth procedure necessary to be a Christian, which was open to all without reservation, was the public avowal and militant practice of that faith, as borne witness to in Paul's letters and life after the event of truth occurred. The event of truth is therefore a discovery, an uncovering or unveiling of a new creation, to which the procedures we then invent express our corresponding fidelity. And a new truth may be creatively discovered in this sense and remained faithful to, according to Badiou, in science, in art, in love, and in politics—which is where he places Saint Paul's case of a new form of militancy that founds the Western sense of universalism. For Badiou, by the way, Saint Paul largely rejects the discourses of Greek philosophy, Jewish law, and his own mystical vision. However that may be, we can say, following Badiou's lead, that a new truth may be a new law in science, a new style or experimental form in art, a new love in our erotic lives, or a political revolution, and its sphere of operation is, of course, human culture.

If, as Paul de Man brilliantly argued, crisis is endemic to the critic's office of criticism, Badiou's ontological poetics of truth in *Being and Event* may just provide us with a significantly new formulation of what we can do.

2

FIGURES OF THE VOID

On the Subject of Truth and the Fundamentalist Imagination

WHAT FOLLOWS IS an encounter between the most classically rationalist imagination among today's philosophers and the most stereotypically irrational of religious imaginations. I have staged this encounter for several reasons. First, I enjoy the sparks that often fly when such things do all too rarely occur. Admittedly, this is my aesthetic perversity at work. Second, I am interested in developing the ontology of the subject in its relationship to truth that can bridge the gap between reason and imagination in their extreme forms. "Why?" you might ask. Who cares? We know that there is no subject or should not be, and even if there is, and we cannot shame it out of existence, yet we must ignore it, as any attention will serve only to preserve it for a little while longer. After all, we have seen "the death of Man," "the death of the author," the tumescence of "Western patriarchal culture," have we not?

In fact, the subject does exist. That is all it does. And it exists, as Alain Badiou suggests, in a way that leads either to revolutionary change or to the betrayal of all revolutionary hopes. There is no middle ground. Either we work for revolution or we work against it, whether we know that or not. We must choose. This is my third and final reason, then.

So, to me, we need an ontology of the subject, a study of the being of the subject, precisely as a guide (and not a guillotine), so that we may know how best to choose in any particular situation what there is to be done.

TRUTH HAPPENS. At least according to Alain Badiou it does.[1] Here is how he conceives of the happening of truth: Any grouping of elements, as in set theory, may be thought of as a situation. What defines the situation as distinctive from any other is the structure of counting that selects the elements to be included in it. We never speak of pure multiplicities but always of collections, whose members we select for inclusion according to a principle of selection that then automatically structures that situation. All the balls that are red, all the people who are white, all the ocean vistas that are blue—these are easy examples, whose principle of selection is clear.

Badiou goes on, of course, to complicate this simple picture. Within each such situation or "set," there is not only a principle of counting and selection at work but also something that eludes or is excluded by the principle, on principle, as it were. As Kurt Gödel demonstrated, any such part not counted and presented as a member belonging to the set is nonetheless antithetically the set in question and its elements. In my previous examples, all based on color, the parts in the situations that cannot be counted in this way—the object features of the situation, say—are still in the situation, even though they are not of it, according to the logic of this particular count. Nonetheless, these uncounted, specifically uncountable, parts are the basis for the formation and functioning of the respective situations: like the servants, say, that make possible a class society, or the subatomic particle waves that constitute the objects that bear the colors. Such incommensurable parts—incommensurate with respect to the principle of selection of the count structuring the set—are said by Badiou to "exist on the edge of the void" and function, when society is the set or situation in question, very much like what Jacques Rancière terms "the part of no part." These nonmember parts of any situation I like to think of, somewhat fancifully perhaps, as "figures of the void."

By this idea Badiou means the following: in set theory, the formal constitution of any situation (also termed "State" by Badiou in a punning reminder of his theory's ramifications) depends on the inclusion of the set of zero (the "zeta" set, named after the Greek letter used to designate it) among its elements; this empty set is the first item counted in any set, made up of any type of elements, structured by any principle of selection. On this foundation, no set can be said to contain itself as one of its members, and so an irrational infinite regress may be avoided. Following the famous Riemann hypothesis, as elaborated by Paul Cohen in *Set Theory and the Continuum Hypothesis,* Badiou claims that in any situation, the nontrivial "zetas," those empty or null sets significantly defining the set, collect along the critical line of the plane, thereby marking the set spatially at its *fault line.*

The set of all apple trees, for example, contains as its first member the nothing, the zero, the void, the empty or null set. The latter contains none of the elements contained in the first set, hence the term *the null set.* This means that, under the label of the null set, all the parts that found the situation or set but that cannot be presented as elements or members of that situation or set due to the particular principle of selection at work may be formally represented. All structured situations like sets include at their base this null set, which represents what is excluded from the count, creating the particular set or situation. Thereafter, in counting the rest of the designated elements (such as apple trees) in the particular set, the null set reproduces itself as the count continues. As the first element counted in the set, the number one refers to the null set. The number two consists in this number one plus the first of the elements designated and included as a member of the set, the number three is the null set plus the number two plus the next element, and so on. Each set member is generically multiple, since it incorporates itself and at least the null set, just as every subsequent number in a sequence of numbers must include the number one (the null set, you will recall, is always counted as the first item) as its basis.

At the same time, the parts not counted and presented by the principle of selection for the set are automatically consigned by the principle of selection to a position in the situation or state that Badiou characterizes, as we have seen, more specifically as existing "on the edge of the void." They are not simply precluded from any consideration. What is excluded from the set is also foundational to the set, and it is represented in the set by the null set. When truth happens, there is an event, a significant conflict between the set's presentational and representational functions, thereby exposing the function of the null set. This exposure of what Badiou, after Lacan, calls "the real" of the situation throws the situation shortly into formal chaos. The solidity and position of all numbers of the situation have been called into question. All members are disclosed to be split between what the member represents in belonging to the set and the null set that stands as this member's and indeed the entire set's fundamental basis. Faced suddenly by the infinity of possibilities the set must preclude in order to constitute itself (all those "zetas" the null set formally presents but materially forecloses), a crisis ensues.

What once seemed impossible, indeed a prospect of infinite possibilities, excluded in principle in advance, irrupts into view out of the void, and this radical prospect of infinity appears to be, counterintuitively, the most possible, for better or worse. Badiou argues that, as Cohen has shown, the nontrivial "zetas," in marking the fault line of the set's structural formation, function like Lacan's "the real," and all disavowed elements must be foreclosed substantially, to make the set or situation cohere. In other words, the null set reveals the *incommensurate* infinite set. In response to the exposure of the null set turning into a revelation of the infinite set, the mind often reacts defensively, returning to established elements in the situation to maintain a familiar sense of self and world.

One's attitude to this crisis in and of the situation depends both on the position one occupies in the previously reigning situation and on one's judgment about that situation and the places of oneself and others in it. It is out of this anarchic crisis that revolutions can occur. And they do occur as events of truth. A totally unpredictable experience of the void of any situation, inspiring the impossible of that situation to appear suddenly possible—this is "the real" of any situation. This experience of the real happens, giving rise to a statement or proclamation of the truth of this experience, which is to guide the further emergence and formation of the new situation.

Any situation, structured by a principle of selection that arbitrarily counts its members as belonging to it, is founded necessarily upon the void and excludes the infinitude of alternative possibilities. It may suffer the event of truth. If so, it thereby gives rise to the subject of that truth event in a way that calls into radical question the terms of the situation. This subject of truth identifies itself not with the situation or its negation but with the proclamation of the truth event per se, which is freely offered and addressed to all without any coercion or sense of personal or group ownership or derivation.

I suppose Badiou's best example of his theory of truth events and truth procedures is that of Pauline Christianity.[2] Paul's visionary experience on the road to Damascus releases into the situation of the early church new possibilities. Paul offers this truth and witness to all: namely, that regardless of their satisfaction of the established law of ritual and belief, the early church's principle of selection, both Gentile and Jew, Pagan and Philosopher, can indeed become members belonging to the situation. Suddenly, what counts in the counting of people in this situation has, unpredictably, been changed by Paul's new universalizable truth.

Such radical contingency is an important part of Badiou's conception of truth as the happening of an event that is rather like Heidegger's conception of truth. But it derives immediately from the Lacanian conception of the unconscious, which appears only in symbolic breakdown, failure, and then fleetingly in a momentary pulse of an imaginary opening that will be closed by the new—or at least the next—symbolic formation or principle of selection that follows, whether in fidelity to the truth of the event or not.

Admittedly, at a first critical glance, this conception of truth as event is strangely static and one-dimensional. What is the dynamic component of it? Mere blind luck? Passive breakdown? In addition, is there only ever one principle of selection at work in a situation? In his most recent work, Badiou attempts to address his critics by formulating what he calls "logics of appearance" for his own ontology of truth as event.[3] For this occasion, I intend to follow my own logic of appearance, based on a revision of certain psychoanalytic notions, which I find to be novel conceptions of structure and event.

The most necessary feature of any situation must be the repetition of the count. The structure of any situation functions actively as a counting operation, as a policing of the "economic" identity of the situation. Whether we think of this in terms of a group situation or a subject's psychic economy, any situation or state, as such, repeatedly counts, that is, inspects and approves authoritatively, its elements as belonging or not belonging, as excludable or as ignorable. The more these ignorable elements increase, the more that must be excluded, but increasingly the more that cannot be. Consequently, the more unstable the structuring, the ever more volatile the situation, the more explosive the event of collapse, and the more shocking the emergence of new, previously unthinkable possibilities will be. If we introduce "overdetermination" into this basic crisis situation (with only one principle of selection in the counting operation), then we can propose that there is more than one principle of selection for membership in any particular situation or set, even if one selection principle remains predominant or "hegemonic." We also recognize that we add another dynamic and potentially explosive factor. The real of this crisis now beckons. Its subjective warning signal is, of course, anxiety.

The logic of appearance for the event of truth is thus like the logic of overdetermination and repetition-compulsion in anxiety neurosis. An important reason that I want to make use of such psychoanalytic logic is that Lacanian psychoanalysis includes subjectivity and comes closest of the human sciences to modeling for subjectivity the logic of self-regulating physical systems (whether living or not), which function very much in this manner, without self-defeatingly doing away with subjective agency altogether. The subject of truth is "the real" of any situation, its critical fault line. As individual, dual, or collective agent, the subject of truth exists in the practices that seek to remain faithful to the new truth, which names the new principle of selection for the situation, as in the case of Paul's visionary practices of witnessing and recruitment, as they reveal the emerging universality of the Christian message. Psychoanalytic theory, elaborating Badiou, thus enables me to propose a viable, rational ontology of the subject within nature.

Moreover, even without the importation of other situations into the field of response of the first situation, that is, even without the essential conflict of any politics, any dynamic system, which is what a situation or state must be, is open to the possibility of its own "internal" politics of self-destruction. The sheer number of elements formally included and excluded (yet still in the situation), the mounting number of principles of selection (overdetermination), the accelerating rhythm of any count, the irruption of conflicts, and the prospect of radical incommensurability—all these things may inhere in any situation, reproducing the subjective existential "mood" of anxiety.

But once we open this analytic model of truth as event to the antagonistic interplay of politics as we know it especially today, the occasions for a critical truth event grow by leaps and bounds, which is also why the policing operations usually can become more subtly violent, complex, and far-reaching in their repressive functions. Anxiety (as I demonstrate in the next chapter) also increases exponentially. Bush's "War on Terror," in this respect, is a good case in point, even as it remains perhaps even cruder than past episodes in American history of this type. However that may be, threatened with collapse from both within and without, any situation is always fraught with truth as an event.

For our purposes, here's what may be said to happen when a truth event happens, based on my adaptation of Badiou's views. Both from within a situation and without—and this distinction is often analytically hard to make, even as in practice it may be made all the time, irrationally and violently—the conflicts and incommensurability of elements are included in any overdetermined, anxiety-ridden count. Those excluded and expelled (as well as those excluded and consigned to existence on the edge of the void or null set) remain at the heart of any situation and the impossible prospect of infinite possibilities (or the infinite set) previously un-thought (because uncountable) by the situation in its own particular ways.

TODAY, THANKS TO global capitalist modernity, we all live in situations that are more or less open to the specter of imminent collapse. The fundamentalist imagination is one of the major "radical" reactions to this threatening apparition. Courage, as opposed to anxiety, would be another possible response to this ever-imminent irruption of the real.

There remain significant debates on the idea that fundamentalisms of all types from around the world are essentially reactions to the destructive spread of capitalist modernity that make selective use of traditional religious elements and cultural values for political purposes. Nonetheless, this view is the majority scholarly position that, following the editors of a recent five-volume set *The Fundamentalism Project*, I will also take.[4] In taking this view, I do not intend to suggest that I believe capitalist modernity is the only global agent of radical change in our epoch. However, in the postwar period, it certainly has been the major dominant force inspiring the many episodes of nationalist and/or fundamentalist reactions. Of course, what may effectively challenge its empire of dissolution remains to be seen.

I want to propose, then, that when capitalist modernity enters the scene of a traditional culture, it not only exposes the null set of that situation—thereby also releasing the uncannily alluring prospect of infinite possibilities, but precisely because it is based on counting in statistical procedures and outlooks—it also transforms the hegemonic value system of the traditional situation to the point of nonrecognition and endless displacement. Members of the traditional culture can all count, potentially, on being discounted and so relegated to being "people of the void," insofar as they are aboard or not aboard the supposed gravy train of capitalist modernity. Capitalist modernity thus functions like a truth event for traditional cultures, wherever they may be located and however they are functioning. Into the already overdetermined and fraught situation of always imminent crisis for a group, capitalist modernity intervenes, at the very least, like the last straw and, most often, like a bomb, transforming its members into the literally or socially symbolic "shameful" forms of the dead.

What the editors of *The Fundamentalist Project* call "the fundamentalist imagination" is, then, a response in religious and cultural spheres first of all to this new crisis situation in their traditional ways of life.[5] Such a purely reactionary response may then take political forms, but it also essentially remains a religious and cultural movement. So-called fundamentalists react to capitalist modernity by returning to religious and cultural traditions and selectively appropriating those elements that, with fitting revision, they feel meet the needs of the critical situation, so that they may not become "people of the void," that is, may not become those elements that are not recognized by the new, often actively hostile principle of selection in the emerging situation. All too naturally, fundamentalists want to continue as they are so as to be able to imagine themselves as counting in their world. This is the fundamental feature of what the term *fundamentalist imagination* really means.

From the perspective provided by my adaptation of Badiou on truth as event, the fundamentalists refuse, indeed disavow, the event of the null set irrupting into their world in the form of capitalist modernity, with the accompanying revelation of the infinite set, and so they never experience a new critical truth to which any proclamation of theirs may bear faithful witness. Instead, they must return to their traditions to select elements of what they feel is a better defense against any such experience in the first place. For Badiou, the closer one comes in any situation of destitution, to the edge of the void, to existing as one of the people of void, the more one is in the truth and the truth in one. This is the visionary truth of the newly emerging situation, out of which authentic revolutionary developments may spring to be guided critically by the faithful witnessing of proclamations whose fidelity to the truth event remains strong.

Once again, we may recall as a pertinent example the experience of Saint Paul. His witnessing to the truth event he suffered not only changed his name and identity; it introduced into the new situation of Christianity a universalism and an antinomianism that made it impossible simply to return to ritual laws of observation and membership connected to circumcision, liturgical practice, and visionary prophecy. After Paul, the new truth "Christ is risen!" would be offered to all as a gift of grace that saved all potentially from the double bind of any law-inspired acts of childish transgression. Our faith alone may save us, regardless of what we do or do not do. Of course, the authentically prophetic vision got him in deep trouble with both Jerusalem and Rome and led to his five years of house arrest in Rome before his death from the proverbial "mysterious circumstances."[6] What makes his case exemplary is that rather than remain the passive victim of crisis, anxiety, and cowardice, Paul embraced this revolutionary vision, universalized it by addressing it to all, and impersonalized it by deriving it from no one set of previously existing and would-be hegemonic factions, groups, or sects and their discourses. This is why the Pauline vision generally remains "new" and "revolutionary" even today.

We know that the dominant American form of fundamentalism, which in fact gives its name to global fundamentalisms, entails a discourse that apes this kind of prophetic vision of Saint Paul. Most of this apocalyptic discourse, however, is drawn not from him but from the book of Daniel and the book of Revelation.[7] This discourse, presupposing biblical inerrancy, also proposes that a limited number of saved souls, these Elect, depending on the state of their souls at the time, will be lifted up into heaven during what they call "the Rapture." This will happen just before the End of Days time of tribulations in most accounts; this is what George W. Bush's pre-millennial fundamentalism holds. The Elect may enjoy observing the working out of God's will on Earth as the Antichrist and the faithful remnant left behind to fight the Battle of Armageddon in Jerusalem, when Jesus will return to offer the Jews a final opportunity to believe in him. Those who do not will suffer the same fate as the evil ones helping Satan. Terrible, cataclysmic fire will destroy them. Thereupon a thousand-year reign of peace will follow, until the Earth is transformed back into paradise and God's saints will either return with perfected bodies from heaven or those who died will experience the resurrection of the body just like Jesus.

Some fundamentalists, believing such a comic-book version of apocalypse, think they have to do nothing politically in the world, that they need only await in faith the working out of God's will. The fundamentalists associated with George W. Bush and the Republican Party, by contrast, believe that political intervention in social and cultural policy matters will keep America a good Christian nation and will help to hasten both the Rapture and Armageddon in some unexplained ways.

As we know from Leo Strauss and his disciples' work, despite their espousal of classical rationalism, such a religious movement may be thought of as a perfect reactionary instrument of politics in a modern democracy, in which the rule of the enlightened elite who know the truth—that we need beautiful lies to live—is secured by dispensing religion, purely for administrative and therapeutic purposes, to the masses, who cannot handle any truth.[8] What is so poisonous about this Straussian position is that it parades as classical rationalism what is in reality the rankest of cynical modern nihilisms. It does so in the name of liberal democracy, all the while actively working to pervert and transform all authentic democratic possibilities into the raw materials and instruments for their new situation of neoconservative elite rule. That situation of elite rule is now being instituted before our stunned eyes. Such a situation is strongly supported and enforced, to our ever greater amazement, by the political madness of an increasingly open theocratic populist ideology.

Naturally, a number of explanations for "the fundamentalist imagination" can be offered. For purposes of analytic clarity and immediately relevant topical reference, I focus on American fundamentalism. Nietzschean ressentiment causes it. It is the sudden prospect of social death being experienced by previously secure traditional peoples of one sort or another. It is the populist response of men in traditional patriarchal societies to the changes introduced into their world by capitalist modernity and its stalking horse, liberal democracy. One could multiply the proposed explanations.[9] I would rather concentrate on the dynamics of the situation, as effectively informed by my adaptation of Badiou's theory of the truth event. The situation faced by the prototypical fundamentalists is one in which the inherent instability of this situation is exasperated to the point of collapse and transformation by capitalist modernity. Failing repeatedly to find a suitable place for themselves in the emerging new order, the prototypical fundamentalists react in a dual way. They anxiously and repeatedly return to the roots of their traditions, select those "fundamental" features most adaptable to the fight of the present moment, and embrace the modes of communications and other aspects of capitalist modernity's technological innovations to promote their now fully recognizable agenda.

What fundamentalists resist with all their being, therefore, is their displacement, material and imaginary, which capitalist modernity would introduce into any traditional culture or society. They resist it in a completely double way. In returning to the original documents and doctrines of their traditional belief and value systems, fundamentalists feel especially *empowered,* in fact, to choose selectively among them and to reinterpret them with ruthless abandon, thereby most often perverting their own origins totally. They then exploit the present situation for all the political edge and financial and technological support they can gain for the promotion of their views and their institutionalization as governmental policies. The revisionism of fundamentalists is a fully engaged kind. Jerry Falwell and Pat Robertson, during the 1980s, come to mind as relevant examples here. However, so too do the Nazis and many other individuals and groups since the American and French revolutions in the West and globally. Merely attempting to placate or buy off fundamentalists, then, clearly misses the point. The displacement that capitalist modernity introduces into the traditional context may be radically negative for fundamentalists in the material dimension, but it is always so in the imaginary dimension. Similarly, whether a particular fundamentalist had been in a leading socially symbolic position or not prior to the intervention of capitalist modernity into the situation, his imaginary experience has been shaken up and usually threatens to be transformed for him in impossible ways. Moreover, this dread of imaginary displacement is often intimately tied to the national, religious, and/or ethnic or racial identity of the fundamentalist's community or state, that is, the established community's worldly status.

The Pauline model of the truth event is almost symbolically in a position of advantage when persecuting the first Christians, and then, through his conversion experience, or truth event, Paul plunged (in terms of real and imaginary status) into the abyss. With his antinomianism and universalism, Paul virtually fell off the radar screen of Peter and James in Jerusalem, until it became clear that he had enough of a following among Gentiles who would contribute financially such that Paul had to be compromised with if possible or, if not, then allowed to be charged by Jewish authorities with blasphemy. When he demanded a trial in Rome before the emperor, as was his right as a Roman citizen, he was confined to house arrest until his death. Ironically enough, those in the Jerusalem Church who opposed receiving Paul's Gentile collection won the day, because they argued successfully that these funds were unclean in principle, having been donated by the uncircumcised. Consequently, then, Peter and James lost both Paul as a self-declared "apostle" and his considerable Gentile collection.[10]

These two features—Paul's universalism and antinomianism—are the twin hallmarks of any authentic truth event. Xenophobic particularism of identity and selective literalism of interpretation have no place in the truth event. We bear witness to this event in a freely offered truth statement or proclamation. The event of truth is not only unpredictable and unlikely, but it is also never cowardly imposed by means of physical or psychological violence on others. Rather, in "fear and trembling," a subject arises out of the void, and this subject may be individual or collective, but it is always singular, having no recognizable derivation in the reigning order; and this subject pronounces its fidelity to the truth event of the real that has appeared and disappeared, as in the twinkling of an eye. The Last Judgment and apocalyptic remaking of the world are not events of truth that end time; rather, they are events that restart time, reinaugurate history, subject by singular subject, like a western wildfire. And either these subjects are already people of the void, or, like Saul after he becomes Paul, they soon become so. To put it in rather mock understatement, their situations have changed—radically.

In the following extended quotation from *Saint Paul: The Foundation of Universalism*, not only does Badiou clarify what is the crucial distinction between the truth event that Paul bears witness to and the initially codified doctrine of early Christianity, to be found in the synoptic Gospels; he also thereby offers the definitive difference between the truth event per se and any form of fundamentalism:

> The Pauline reference [to the event] is of a different substance [from the Gospels]. The event is not a teaching; Christ is not a master; disciples are out of the question. . . . The Christ-event establishes the authority of a new subject path over future eras. . . . [There is] a community of destiny in that moment in which we have to become "a new creature." That is why we need to retain of Christ only what ordains this destiny, which is indifferent to the particularities of the living person: Jesus is resurrected; nothing else matters, so that Jesus becomes like an anonymous variable, a "someone" devoid of predicative traits, entirely absorbed by his resurrection. The pure event is reducible to this: Jesus died on the cross and was resurrected. This event is "grace" (*kharis*). Thus, it is supernumerary relative to all this and presents itself as pure givenness. As subject to the ordeal for the real, we are henceforth constituted by eventual grace. The crucial formula—which, it must be noted, is simultaneously a universal address—is: *ou gar este hup noman all'hupo kharin*, "for

you are not under the law, but under grace" (Rom. 6:14). A structuring of the subject [is accomplished] according to a "not . . . but" through which it must be understood . . . a becoming rather than a state [results]. The subject of the new era is a "not . . . but." . . . *It is precisely this form that bears the universal* [original italics].[11]

No literalism, particularism, or exceptionalism can successfully operate in the context of this division of the subject into the "not" of the null set and the "but" of the infinite set of the event of truth, a "not . . . but" subjective formation, which also breaks history in two. Just as the key elements that mark Pauline Christianity as an authentic truth event for Badiou are its universalism and antinomianism, so, too, the key elements that mark any fundamentalism are precisely the opposites of these traits: a xenophobic particularism of identity and a literalism of interpretation of the law establishing the outward signs of that identity. The repeated accusation of un-Americanism and the repeated insistence on biblical inerrancy by our homegrown fundamentalism demonstrates how far it is from the Pauline Christian, or indeed any, truth event.

Granted this critical distinction, why is it that millions of Americans nonetheless declare beliefs, in biblical inerrancy and pre-millennial rapture, the traits distinguishing one major form of fundamentalism from another, that are clearly so irrational? Are we to assume that all of them are certifiably insane or perversely proud of their chosen ignorance? While madness or ignorance can explain many things, in this instance they can tell us nothing of use. In order to provide some insight into the possible reason for why fundamentalism has been perceived as possible in our current situation, I will underscore the major critical features of Badiou's model of the truth event in preparation for discussing what still to my mind is the best analysis of the religious complex I know, Freud's reading of the psychotic Dr. Schreber's *Memoirs of My Nervous Illness*.[12]

Badiou proposes that those who exist in any situation on the edge of the null set, because they do not count in that situation, for whatever reason, are exposed to the always possible vision of the essential destitution and volatility of it or any situation. The contingent ways people respond to this ontological vision of the essential destitution and volatility of it or any situation appear striking in our age of capitalist modernity. This impersonal, anonymous, atheistic mathematical sublime is precisely the ontological revelation that fundamentalists refuse by disavowing, even as they approach it in the mistaken terms of their own personal sinfulness or errancy. The true vision of pure destitution and total nihilism, disavowed or foreclosed from memory, like the prospects of symbolic castration, necessarily returns from the unconscious, in the bizarrely distorted forms of the deranged fantasies of a partially *healing* paranoid psychosis. This is Freud's most original insight: "*What we take to be the production of the illness, the formation of the delusion, is in reality the attempt at a cure, the reconstruction*"[13] of the self's lost relationship to its world. After suffering a tremendous blow to his self-regard, Schreber cannot face his symbolic investiture as judge in his traditional cultural situation and abandons his emotional investments in people and objects. As he begins to project his paranoid fantasies of being used as a woman by his psychiatrist—which is soon superseded by the grander, if more blasphemous, fantasy of being transformed into a woman so that he may pleasure god and bear him a new race of superior beings who, like him, can think exciting thoughts constantly—Schreber is actually, according to Freud's brilliant insight, not sinking deeper into paranoid psychosis but rather beginning to recover his relationship—albeit a strange one—to his libidinal objects.

What I am proposing, then, is that the fundamentalist imagination is an attempted act of recovery of this sort on the part of believers who live on the edge of psychosis all the time. The following is the conversion narrative of Elder Walter Evans of the Primitive Baptists of the Blue Ridge Mountains of North Carolina.[14] Before recounting it, Elder Evans explains that he had always "felt so much of my time in my life, like a stranger," especially when he observed religious rites. "As for me, I got nothing out of [anything]" (121). This alienation was radical, and nearly total, except for periodic binges of booze and sex in town. Elder Evans before conversion was dead to the world, virtually psychotically withdrawn.

As his self-destructive pathology lifts, at least partially, with his conversion (the deadpan tone of his narrative is a sign of this partiality), Elder Evans continues his conversion tale:

> It was on Tuesday night while standing at the back of the house [watching a service my father insisted I attend] that I felt a strong power arrested my heart and soul to the extent my body trembled under the weight like a leaf on a tree shaken by a mighty wind. A voice from somewhere, a still voice taut with power, said: "You are lost without God or hope in the world." (122)

Elder Evans recalls how he sank on the mourner's bench, inconsolable by his parents or anyone else, convinced that his sins were too great to be forgiven, when that same still voice taut with power announced, "Your sins are all forgiven," and thereupon, "Before the song [of the congregation] was ended, a call or strong impression came to me.... O, how I desired to tell what the Lord had done for me. I was in a new world" (123). You may recall that the voice speaking to Paul in his Damascus Road vision asks a critical question, but it does not promise, as Elder Evans's voice in his vision does, any final solution.

Rather than living with the symbolic and imaginary destitution of his life as a stranger in the world on the edge of the void, as one of the people of the void in the situation of modern America, Elder Evans is seized by the already formulated and elaborated fundamentalist mythos of his historical context, and so he may again begin to relate to his world, albeit only through a highly limited and stylized mode of expression. Elder Evans is clearly no Saint Paul, an inspired master of visionary paradox and a martyr to his own inventive theology. Like Schreber, however, Elder Evans's conversion experience reconciles him to his father and mother and his locality, and it opens the door to his assuming a leading position there. Schreber, having failed the crisis of symbolic investiture by going mad, nonetheless then became a cause célèbre in the well-established discipline of general psychiatry at the time when Freud appropriated his memoirs for his own original purposes. In Badiou's terms, fundamentalism is a step up (and back) in socially symbolic space from becoming one of the people of the void. Like William Blake's title character in the *Book of Thel,* who, rather than encounter the terrible void of the grace of experience, hastily returns to the unreality of her stereotypical pastoral abstraction, the fundamentalist imagination would rather embrace an accredited form of madness than discover its own potentially revolutionary truth.

In conclusion, I would suggest that the fundamentalist imagination is what we may think of as the most common, socially acceptable form of "healing" madness in modern America.

3

"THE CRY OF ITS OCCASION"

On the Subject of Truth, Or the Terror in Global Terrorism

THIS CHAPTER will skirt the edges of literature. My primary concern here is to outline a broadly Lacanian theory of the subject of truth. This subject should be able to resist, on the one hand, assimilation to the law of the global economy and, on the other, subjective identification with already established, so-called minority groups. Such a subject, in short, would be "new," even revolutionary, with respect to the present moment. In this respect, I will be following the lead of Alain Badiou.

So, to begin with (and for all of what follows), I want to borrow as the motto for this chapter a formulation from Badiou's *Saint Paul*: "A subject without identity, a law without support."[1] Although this formulation may sound nihilistic, such is not the case. Without going into all the details of Badiou's analysis of Saint Paul's letter, I will start here by referring to the problem Badiou poses, to which this catchy formulation is ironically the solution.

Badiou is in search of a viable militant figure of the subject in its relationship to truth. What are this figure's invariantly resistant traits? According to Badiou, we currently live in a world where the abstract homogeneity of the global market economy (one counts only if one submits to being counted) and its rapid and devastating flows of capital (and all the rest) define the general parameters for an oppositional array of preestablished group identities. No one such identity, nor any combination of them, can determine for him the militant subject of truth. The landscape of differential identity types, in fact, constitutes the established terrain upon which the abstract homogenization of the global market, ironically enough, can exercise its powers for ever greater profits. Here is Badiou on the topic:

> Both processes [of subjectivization and commodification] are perfectly intertwined. For each identification (the creation or cobbling together of identity) creates a figure that provides a material for its investment by the market. There is nothing more captive, so far as commercial investment is concerned, nothing more *amenable* to the invention of new figures of monetary homogeneity, than a community and its territory or territories. The semblance of a nonequivalence is required so that equivalence itself can constitute a process. What inexhaustible potential for mercantile investments in this upsurge—taking the form of communities demanding recognition and so-called cultural singularities—of women, homosexuals, the disabled, Arabs! And these infinite combinations of predicative traits, what god-send! Black homosexuals, disabled Serbs, Catholic pedophiles, moderate Muslims, married priests, ecologist yuppies, the submissive unemployed, prematurely aged youth! Each time a social image authorizes new products, specialized magazines, improved shopping malls, "free" radio stations, targeted advertising networks, and finally, heady "public debates" at peak viewing times. Deleuze put it perfectly: capitalist deterritorialization requires a constant reterritorialization. Capital demands a permanent creation of subjective and territorial identities in order for its principle of movement to homogenize its space of action: identities, moreover, that never demand anything but the right to be exposed in the same way as other to the uniform prerogatives of the market. The capitalist logic of the general equivalent and the identitarian and cultural logic of communities or minorities form an articulated whole. (*SP* 10–11)

To put it in other, slightly less satiric terms, the global economy is the literal default position for the absence of any accessible real for the diverse "minorities" whose cultures (or so-called subcultures) constitute the cynically recognizable mirages of our global culture. The contemporary subject may declare the truth of its identity-theme, whatever it may be, and its distinctive (if too often exclusive, brand-like) cultural affiliation, but it cannot declare any universalizable truth. Such a truth of the subject is one that arises out of the unpredictable experience of the real; it has no determinative source in the symbolic order, and no purely imaginary phantasm can capture or captivate it for narrow partisan or sectarian interests.

In the current context, the global economy and its culture operate *as* the ultimate horizon of thinking for all and *at* the most intimate levels of the single one, that of the subject's relationship to itself. What are permitted are only the prefabricated identities or minor group imaginaries. This is the case so long as the groups accept their grounding in the global market's rule of law, presumably based on principles of democratic tolerance, but actually based in the powers of the security forces of the nation and the international economic order. The law and order of global modernity is the provocative basis for all the reactive types of supposedly transgressive, oppositional imaginary identities.

The foundation of universalism for late capitalist global culture, in short, is not the subject's relationship to its truth, which it declares and offers to all—the prototypical situation of the Pauline Christian. It is, rather, the mindless, passionless operations of the global market as it rotates one after another subject-type into position as the latest object of commodification and control. Such an ersatz façade of universalism is the demonic parody of any potentially authentic universalism. According to Badiou, the latter is always a *singular* universalism: the subject in question has no relationship of derivation to what went before the event of truth it passionately undergoes and to which it bears faithful witness in its proclamation. As such, the authentic subject of truth testifies to the absence of any law touching its being, even the law of its own supposed intellectual autonomy. Like Saul becoming Paul "on the Road to Damascus," the subject of truth has no relationship to commodification and control by means of the market. The event of truth and its subject is incommensurate with all *established* orders, even as it cuts across any such order.

Consequently, this means that no one subject or group under the hegemony of global capitalism can stand in a creative relationship to the truth of the real. In fact, each must accept the alibis of the global system and the utopian or merely fantastic fictions of this system's ideology or its group's reactive imaginary. No new revolutionary social formation, therefore, can emerge from such a situation of essentially captive audiences of the present world-system. The subject's relationship to the declaration of truth is at best reduced to the status of a reality television show, in which the participants perform their identities for millions of others vicariously, and often viciously, to enjoy. The military police at Abu Ghraib, who with sadomasochistic antics videotaped and photographed themselves torturing prisoners to the point of total abjection of all concerned, would be the logical extension of such practices as regularly grace *Fear Factor*. Time to eat the worms, boys and girls!

For Badiou, Saint Paul represents the figure par excellence of the militant radical subject in its relationship to the declaration of truth. Badiou calls him "the poet-thinker of the event" (*SP* 2). This is because Saint Paul proposes truth procedures that are antinomian—against all established law—and anonymous—no group identity pre-owns the truth: hence, precisely, "a subject without an identity, a law without support" (*SP* 5). Saint Paul subtracts identity per se from the law of the Roman Empire in the subject's relationship to preestablished truths of any kind, whether of a Jewish or Hellenistic sort. Here is, again, how Badiou puts it:

> Paul's general procedure is the following: if there has been an event [designated as such, "Christ is risen!"] and if truth consists in declaring [it] and then in being faithful to this declaration, two consequences ensue. First, since truth is evental, or of the order of what occurs, it is singular. It is neither structural, nor axiomatic, nor legal. No available generality [such as Empire of any kind] can account for it, nor [can it] structure the subject who claims to follow in its wake. Consequently, there cannot be a law of truth. Second, truth being inscribed on the basis of a declaration that is in essence subjective, no pre-constituted subset [or group] can support it; nothing communitarian or historically established can lend its substance to the process of truth. [That is,] Truth is diagonal relative to every communitarian subset; it neither claims authority from, nor (this is obviously the most delicate point) constitutes any identity. It is offered to all, or

addressed to everyone, without a condition of belonging being able to limit this offer or this address. (*SP* 14)

Badiou does not accept the fable of Christian salvation history that Saint Paul uses to fill out the form of these truth procedures. His interest is not in the particulars of doctrine but in the relationship of the subject to its truth. Can the subject, without cowardly resorting to physical violence, universalize it or not? Badiou does have his own theory of "grace," as the secularization of the infinite, but that will have to become my subject on another occasion. I will suggest in my conclusion, however, that the revolutionary artist and this subject's "cry of its occasion" may best incarnate such a "graceful" infinitude.

As an example of these truth procedures at work, I want to present a famous passage from Saint Paul about the Law's relationship to transgression. This comes from Saint Paul's most influential letter, the Epistle to the Romans:

> I would not have known wrongdoing if it were not for the Law. For, I would not have known desire if the Law did not say, "you shall not desire." But wrongdoing, taking its opportunity through the commandment, effected in me every desire. For apart from the Law, wrongdoing is dead. And without the Law I was once alive, but when the commandment came wrongdoing sprang to life, and I died, and the commandment—the commandment issued for life—this was found to be for me a commandment for death. For wrongdoing, taking its opportunity through the commandment, deceived me utterly and through it killed me. . . . For what I am effecting, I do not know. For what I want—that's not what I do; but what I hate—that's what I do. And if what I don't want—that's what I do—then I say "Yes" to the Law, and agree it is fine. And now it is no longer me effecting this, but the wrongdoing that lives in me. For I know that the good does not live in me, I mean in my flesh. For to want it, that is close to hand, but to effect what is fine—that is not. For I didn't do what I want, the good; but what I don't want, the bad—that is what I do. And if what I don't want—that's what I do—then it is no longer me that is effecting it, but the wrongdoing that lives in me. So I find the Law, for me who wants to do what is fine—I find that for me what is bad

> is close to hand. I share the delight in the Law of God, in my inner person; but I see another law in my members, waging war against the Law of my mind and taking me prisoner in the Law of wrongdoing which is in my members. What a wretch am I! Who will deliver me from the body of this death?—But thanks be to God through Jesus Christ our Lord! There is now no condemnation for those who are in Christ Jesus. For . . . the Spirit of Life in Christ Jesus has freed [us all] from the Law of Sin and of death. (Romans 7:7–25)[2]

Saint Paul speaks in anguish and joy here about the conflict between laws: the old Law of Moses, which determines the mind, and the Law of Transgression (wrongdoing, or "Sin"), which determines the flesh, the body, and its unruly members. And he does this speaking as if in his own voice, making his own case the great prototype of all possible cases, assimilating to this figure of himself in his text the biblical archetypes of Moses and Adam in the process. (I cannot help hearing prophetic echoes here, too, of Freud and Foucault, among others, on the unconscious, repression, and the ironic law of transgression.)

Saint Paul, I believe, is internalizing, incorporating, incarnating, in the persona of this address—an address offered to the Roman converts, mostly Gentiles, but also to all and sundry pagans and Jews—the central conflict between the Law (any law) and that which it produces: the materials of purely reactive transgression, the unruly members of the flesh, "the body of this death." Neither mind alone, nor body alone, nor mind and body together, can suffice for authentic existence—they only grant, alone or together, the terrible anguish of total self-abjection. Only the entirely uncanny third term and being, the Spirit (or "grace"), may grant this gift of a new creation in oneself.

The Spirit is the unruly phantasm (or specter) of the body of this death transformed, transfigured, in the twinkling of an eye, into the new sign of life ("grace") by the repeated *anxiety for the real*. This is why he can refer to his own private travails as the creative gift of grace. These travails, like that of a woman in labor, constitute a potential representative giving birth to himself, thanks to the penetrating power of the Spirit. In this public confession of his private sufferings, in other words, Saint Paul unveils in his own person the liberating truth of this new faith: "There is now no condemnation for those who are in Christ Jesus. For . . . the Spirit of Life in Christ Jesus has freed you from the Law of Sin and of death."[3] The Spirit of Life joyfully transcends not only the Jewish Law (or any such law) but in the grace of the Spirit the very idea of Law itself.

In Badiou's mathematical formulation, as the reader will recall, the subject of truth emerges always from a particular situation whose state (often maintained by the State, in the big sense) contains what is missing from its elements in a form analogous both to the null (or empty) set and to the infinite set in set theory. This "void" or impossible "infinitude" emerges out of the particulars, even the peculiarities, of a specific situation. Experienced as the real of this situation, a subject arises in "fear and trembling," in a condition of radical anxiety or terror, to which as its real this subject seeks to maintain its fidelity. As such, this subject prophetically declares the truth of the event as the event of truth appropriate to the initial situation, even if necessarily constructed and recognized as being so, retroactively, by posterity. All symptoms, as seen from the perspective of the dominant order of society or that of a person's routine fantasies, are marks of veracity and fidelity to such truth, its stigmata. The visionary proclamation of the subject of truth is at once an authentically discursive and bodily gesture: Saint Paul's "vision" from Romans would be, for Badiou, a good case in point of an essentially visionary literary discourse. According to him, the discourse of politics, science, art, and love provides the raw materials for what he calls "the sutures" that philosophy requires to compose itself into the source of potentially universal truths. We can distinguish each age in the history of philosophy by what it chooses to use as the primary material for its "suture." Our age, so far, has been sutured by the faux art of terror.

The problem with our current global culture of multicultural minority identities, as Badiou has declared, is that hardly any subject feels at all empowered by its imaginary identifications to attempt to universalize, solely by means of its proclamations and existential witnessing, what it takes as its truth. The result has been that the supposed truths of the subject are automatically recognized and confessed to be self-justifying fictions of one person or group. The conditions—material and cultural—of the world-system remain the default position of all. This is true of everyone, it would seem—even terrorists whose activities are not intended, after all, to win over others to their traditional beliefs but rather to eliminate others from the ranks of modernity and its regimes of power, even as they take assiduous enjoyment in that modernity's determining technologies and commodities. The "truth" of terrorism is therefore a purely negative, horrifically literal, self-destructive fiction: it doesn't uplift the other or oneself; it blows both of them up.

According to Frank Lentricchia and Jody McAuliffe in *Crimes of Art and Terror*, avant-garde artists, from Wordsworth to Stockhausen, espouse a similarly perverse negative fiction of their radical formal visions, to the point where they too express a transgressive desire for the apocalyptic destruction of Western culture—I say "too," meaning that these artists share this fundamental transgressive desire with terrorists, whether homegrown like the Unabomber, or bred abroad:

> From romanticism to modernism, these [avant-garde] movements consciously presented themselves as revolutionary and sought to shake up—and even overturn—the order of the West. We find that disturbing events of violence and terror—including the events of September 11—are in many ways governed by a logic that grows out of romantic tradition, as life imitates art with a vengeance and real terrorists take their inspiration from books. Transgressive desire is again and again on display: encouraging us to reexamine our presuppositions about our artistic heritage and, above all, challenging our easy assumption that art is something good and at worst benign.[4]

It is, then, no wonder that the psychology of anxiety cannot help defining the daily lives of people. I want to propose that, given the rule of the ideology of terrorism under global capitalism, anxiety must saturate the field and horizon of existence to such an extent that no possibility of change can even begin to be imagined without invoking anxiety. Consequently, we all become like swimmers treading water over twenty thousand fathoms, or like Saul in the anguished instant before he sees the light of the real and thereby becomes Paul.

Anxiety, of course, is the affective response to the sense of trauma or its imminent, if unspecified, approach. We know this from Freud's last major work on the subject, *Inhibitions, Symptoms, and Anxiety* (1926).[5] As inspired by trauma, anxiety is the experience of helplessness in the face of the sudden emergence of unpredictable and overwhelming stimuli, whether from without or within, whether experienced individually or communally in groups. We may call this form of anxiety the event of anxiety. As in the homeopathic treatment of severe allergies, a little dose of such signal anxiety may go a long way to a cure or at least to being a therapeutic palliative.

Although Freud officially lays to rest in this book his earliest psychoanalytic conception of neurotic anxiety as the transformation of excess libido (due to repression) into anxiety, I want to retain it, if only for the idea of the transformation of an excess of one thing into something else, as a partial therapeutic release. This would then be the third type of anxiety, anxiety as a partially transformative safety-valve mechanism: currents of energy become like released gases (sublimations) of some kind. (Whether such partial sublimations are repressive forms or not, or just the psychic equivalent of breaking wind, I am leaving open at this time.)

We can reasonably conclude from this, I think, that the vent of anxiety as trauma directly refers to the present; the prospect of anxiety, or signal anxiety, would refer to the future; and anxiety as this magical safety valve would reference the past, as a dimension where unwanted levels of tension have built up and are demanding release. This insistent call for release would be either (according to Freud's disavowed theory) via sexual activity or via any of its elementary substitutes, including dispersing quanta of anxiety via symptomatic displacements of one sort or another, like hysterical diarrhea or vomiting. As uncannily predicted by Kierkegaard and phenomenologically demonstrated by Heidegger, anxiety, for Freud, too, is thus deeply entangled with the human experience of temporality as an essentially objectless horizon of uncanny dread.[6] The latest discussions in empirical/psychobiological circles, surprisingly enough, concur with such a conclusion, as found in psychoanalytic and phenomenological theories, namely, that there is a deep connection between anxiety and the traumatic experience of time.[7]

Naturally, the present form of anxiety, event anxiety, in its sense of helplessness, does refer to the past, the past of infancy, when we were all helpless, as well as to the subsequent repetitions of such feelings of helplessness, up to the emergence of the latest moment of event anxiety. Similarly, anxiety as a prospective signal addresses not only the future but the very idea of becoming itself, as any kind of change or new emergence, and, as such, strongly alludes to the present (and its immediate past) as continuing static conditions that the organism desperately strives to maintain. Finally, anxiety as a magical safety valve looks forward to or anticipates a future as a return to homeostasis and to a present of mounting excitation, as well as to a past as the repeated run-up to such a present situation.

I have sketched out this anatomy of anxiety to argue that anxiety (in any or all of its forms) is, in the post-9/11 world, now being called "terror." Terror, of course, has been elicited for a long time as a response to horror, via gothic tales and movies, and has been analyzed and exploited by everyone from Edmund Burke to Alfred Hitchcock, just to name a few of the more respectable figures. But terror, when occasioned by violently radical political acts, is what anxiety, with its newly emergent global reach, most prominently and immediately has become for us in our post-9/11 world. In other words, terror and terrorism now constitute "a geopolitics of anxiety."

In sum, anxiety, in its three forms of traumatic event, prospective signal, and magical safety valve, is so entangled with temporality as it is experienced by human beings that it must appear in overlapping linear and nonlinear ways, simultaneously, which means its structure cannot be easily mapped. This problem with representing anxiety, which Freud's book largely and repeatedly demonstrates, according to editor James Strachey, makes discussing analytically its latest political manifestations as "terror" extremely difficult.[8]

As is always the case when dealing with anxiety, then, one must return to it. Badiou, in a journal entry dated April 18, 1977, published recently, develops Lacan's conception of anxiety by relating it to the super-ego via the bizarre phenomenon of the subject's helpless power of anxiously preceding itself. Badiou thus focuses on Lacan's revisionary analysis of anxiety in relationship to the real of the super-ego. Here is Lacan on the super-ego, as cited by Badiou:

> The super-ego is at one and the same time the law and its destruction. As such, it is speech itself, the commandment of law, in so far

as nothing more than its root remains. The law is entirely reduced to something, which cannot even be [fully] expressed, like the You must [of the pure imperative], which is speech deprived of all its meaning. It is in this sense that the super-ego ends up by being identified with only what is most devastating, most fascinating, in the primitive experiences of the subject. It ends up being identified with what I call the ferocious figure, the figures which we can link to primitive traumas the child suffered, whatever these are.[9]

The subject experiences anxiety in relationship to this ferocious figure of the super-ego, whose law is a meaningless blank of pure infinite commandment: you must. Badiou argues that because the super-ego gives access to the force of law as it fashions the law's own power to destroy itself, it then is "the first sign of the eternal precedence of the subject to itself" (LD 43). This sign of the super-ego is the often-paralyzing signal of anxiety, with respect to all the subject's possible futures. The engulfing real of this infinite prospect of pure futurity invades the subject like a smothering presence without any openings.

Badiou cites Lacan again, this time on anxiety proper:

> Anxiety is a crucial term of reference, because in effect anxiety is that which does not deceive. But anxiety may be lacking. In experience, it is necessary to canalize it and, if I may say so, to take it in small doses, so that one is not overcome by it. This is a difficulty which is similar to that of bringing the subject into contact with the real. (LD 43)

Badiou then further comments on Lacan's theory of anxiety at some length, as follows:

> Anxiety is the result of the submersion by the real, of the radical excess of the real over the lack [of desire in the symbolic order]. It is [thus] the destruction of the symbolic network by what reveals itself, here in the opening, of the unspeakable encounter. [Consequently] it is necessary to channel anxiety's effect, since it destroys the adjustment to the repeatable. It short-circuits . . . the subject [into] the real. Anxiety, then, is the sign of that which in the subject forces [the site of the law's own self-overcoming]. As Lacan says beautifully, anxiety is

nothing but the lack of the lack. But when the lack comes to lack, its metonymic effect is interrupted and a real loss has to start, which is paid for with the ravaging of all symbolic points of reference. Hence anxiety never lies. Destruction must meet the law of lack in order to sweep away deception, the semblant, and the oblivion of oblivion. The super-ego, in so far as it is the ferocious figure, reveals the illegality of the law, as it mandates the absolute absurdity of the You must haunting the subject as its truth of being. (LD 42–43)

Anxiety signals the subject's recognition of this self-destructive transcendence of the law over itself. The subject experiences the self-cancellation of the law as an encounter of the overwhelming presence of the real, the lack of the lack. This lacking lack is what is not lacking when interpellation into the symbolic order is securely if repeatedly in place. With "the ravaging of all symbolic points of reference," however, the subject stands open to the experience of the event of its truth, which it then may declare and offer to all. This "unspeakable encounter" may arise intrapsychically, as the ego's confrontation by the ferocious figure of the super-ego, but also (and in adult life usually at the same time) as one subject's truthful experience of another subject in real love: the ultimate "unspeakable encounter." Of course, the global market culture, the contemporary symbolic order, exists with its imaginary fetishistic commodities precisely to foreclose on the real possibility of such an event of truth for the subject. Consequently, when what is foreclosed upon by the symbolic order returns in the real, it must be the literal "ravaging of all symbolic points of reference," as in the apocalyptic terrorism of modern art and politics courageously discussed by Lentricchia and McAuliffe in their *Crimes of Art and Terror.* The avant-garde artist and the suicidal terrorist, in the context I have been constructing, may thus be seen as the imaginary and symbolic instances (respectively) of what Lacan has called "the ferocious figure," which the super-ego cuts for the anxiety-ridden subject of modernity. The contemporary terrorist impersonates "the ferocious figure" for us.

Badiou, in these journal reflections from 1977, goes on to discuss how the subject may productively appropriate (via analysis) the experience of the real, so as to give birth to a new, even revolutionary, order. "The excess-of-the-real," he declares, "detached [by and in analysis] from its obscure readability in the truth of anxiety, must be able to stretch the symbolic order and not simply to replace what functions as the out-of-place" of the lawless law (LD 52). Presumably, by such sensitive but firm stretching, one may insert the truth of the subject, arising out of the faithful declaration of the event of the real, which is offered to all—not for purposes of the profitable exchange of goods and services, but instead for the purely creative giving's sake. Rather than exploding a bomb as one's truth into the global order of modern culture, therefore, the subject of truth presents to all who are willing to receive it its witnessing to "courage," the graceful gift of such giving, without any reservations, inserting thereby its newly invented proclamation into the matrix of contemporary communications. Out of its repeated anxiety for the real, the subject may live as if each moment were the end of the world or the time of its new birth. This is not, I think, a bad thing, for it can become the real basis for any good that may happen. That is, we can become authentic witnesses to our own proclamations of the spirit of life's repeated triumph over the always-imminent threat of death.

But all this self-transformation, of course, requires personal as well as collective courage, according to Badiou, a virtue that the present age ridicules, when it doesn't ignore it. Courage, for him, is putting anxiety to work:

> Courage is the non-subjection to the symbolic order at the urging of the dissolutive injunction of the real. Arising in response to the excess-of-the-real, courage is identical to anxiety, but as [an absolutely] disruptive [if creative] force.... Through the disruption of communication, courage brings disorder into the symbolic, whereas anxiety is simply the invocation of death. [Courage as strength of mind] relates to the true. The true is the result of a deficiency in the symbolic produced by the [merely transgressive] thrust of the real. From this deficiency the subject derives its force, which is proportional to the measure of its courage in the face of the radical absence of any security. In this [sensitive] situation, the subject loses its name.... [Security] de-subjectifies.... [Security] is not a virtue, but rather the sign of subjective impotence. Anxiety results from the [ferocious] deficiency of the place [in the symbolic order], while courage is the [delicate] assumption of the real by which the place is

productively disrupted. Anxiety and courage share the same causality in a reversible order. Hence a political subject comes into being only by giving rebellion a revolutionary value, by tying destruction [anxiety] to reconstruction [courage]. It will become apparent in the real that every order and every legal injunction, however stable they may seem, end up internally dividing themselves. The Other must let itself be [gracefully] divided into an unknown Other that it never was, and into a Same whose identity it had never [repressively] prescribed. (LD 52–53)

In the admittedly somewhat dark light of Badiou's rather gnomic declarations here, I would like to conclude by suggesting that the "unknown Other," which the "Other must let itself" first "be [gracefully] divided into," is, in fact, what he himself terms in his later meditation on Saint Paul "a subject without identity"; and that the "Same of this Other, "whose identity" the Other "had never [repressively] prescribed," is "a law without support." The array of multicultural minor identities put on display in the global marketplace and their spectral shadowing antithetical doubles, the revolutionary avant-garde artist or the radical suicidal terrorist, all cancel themselves out anxiously and equally in the sudden and unpredictable emergence of the "unknown Other," singularly declared in the subject's courageous proclamation of its truth of imaginative witness, a truth that is offered to all. In other words, rather than anxiously domesticating terror in the sublime prospect of global terrorism, which the security forces of global capitalism may subdue to its repressive purposes, we can instead see that such terror may become what Wallace Stevens, another poet-thinker of the event, already envisions modern poetry as, namely, "the cry of its occasion"—or, in short, the subject of truth itself:

The poem is the cry of the occasion,
Part of the res itself and not about it.
The poet speaks the poem as it is,

Not as it was: part of the reverberation
Of a windy night as it is, when the marble statues
Are like newspapers blown by the wind. He speaks

By sight and insight as they are. There is no
Tomorrow for him. The wind will have passed by,
The statues will have gone back to be things about.

The mobile and the immobile flickering
In the area between is and was are leaves,
Leaves burnished in autumnal burnished trees,

And leaves in whirlings in the gutters, whirlings
Around and away, resembling the presence of thought,
Resembling the presences of thoughts, as if,

In the end, in the whole psychology, the self,
The town, the weather, in a casual litter,
Together, said words of the world are the life of the world.[10]

This whole psychology of self, its "words of the world" that are "the life of the world," does not constitute what Slavoj Žižek recently has prophetically invaded against, some "total availability of the past to its subsequent retroactive rewriting."[11] Instead, the self's "casual litter" of emotionally invested letters constitutes what Žižek proclaims as "the Real of a traumatic encounter whose structuring role in the subject's psychic economy forever resists its symbolic rewriting."[12] In our other terms, that is, the terror in global terrorism is the hard truth of the subject.

Part Two

THE LITERARY CULTURE OF GLOBAL AMERICA

4

GLOBAL AMERICA AND THE
LOGICS OF VISION

THE EMERGENCE of what I call "global America" coincides with the emergence of American literature during the antebellum, so-called American Renaissance, period. As many critics and scholars have remarked, literature in the American context develops at the expense of other genres of writing, such as national narrative, local-color tall tales, romance, chronicles, etc. Literature defines itself as such in dialectical opposition to, and critical negation but also sublimation of, these other modes of writing. During this time, and following the romantic example of late-eighteenth- and earlier-nineteenth-century Britain and especially Germany, imaginative writing sets itself off as a separate world whose internal logic of self-reference apparently takes precedence over its referential power with respect to the social and historical worlds in which it appears. I say apparently because in fact literature constituted as a separate world nonetheless acts as a critique of its time and place by its very existence and its often-critical reflection of and upon the world of its origin.[1]

Ralph Waldo Emerson plays a central role in this constitution of American literature. He does so because he demonstrates most clearly and powerfully the logic of vision that informs this emergence, and nowhere does he perform his demonstration more powerfully than in his famous 1844 essay, "Experience." In this essay, more than others, Emerson invents what I call global America. I take this position knowing full well it stands opposed by the present-day American studies establishment.

What "Experience" demonstrates, precisely, are the morbid preconditions for the birth of this figure of global America. Nothing less than the death of the capacity to be in relationship with people and objects around one that can penetrate and pervade the imaginative being of oneself are required if the ideas of "Experience" are to be enacted. "Experience" demands nothing less than the death of the power to love. Emerson candidly exhibits this precondition with his admission that with the death of his son and namesake Waldo, "two years ago," he had expected, as such a costly price, to be brought "into the reality." I understand his "reality" to mean a deep-seated and penetrating passion. Instead, as fits with all the examples in this essay of the illusory nature of the world and its apparently determinant forces, this experience of the death of his son only proves that "souls never touch their objects," much as bodies, as modern science shows, never touch each other either (167). Here is the famous passage in which Emerson confesses his discovery of this first principle of a terrible logic:

> In the death of my son, now more than two years ago, I seem to have a beautiful estate,—no more. I cannot get it nearer to me. If tomorrow I should be informed of the bankruptcy of my principal debtors, the loss of my property would be a great inconvenience to me, perhaps, for many years; but it would leave me as it found me,—neither better nor worse. So it is with this calamity: it does not touch me: something which I fancied was a part of me, which could not be torn away without tearing me, nor enlarged without enriching me, falls off from me, and leaves no scar. It was caduceus. I grieve that grief can teach me nothing, nor carry me one step into real nature. The Indian who was laid under a curse, that the wind should not blow on him, nor water flow to him, nor fire burn him, is a type of us all. The dearest events are summer-rain, and we the Para coasts that shed every drop. Nothing is left now but death. We look to that with a grim satisfaction, saying, there at least is reality that will not dodge us. . . .[2]

CHAPTER 4 | GLOBAL AMERICA AND THE LOGICS OF VISION

What Emerson displays here is the first principle of a logic of vision that constitutes both American literature as such and what I call global America. It is the "state of mind," as William Blake might put it, that permits capitalism, imperialism, and dreams of Manifest Destiny to flourish with more or less a good conscience. The American dream may very well begin with the acceptance of this awful self-recognition: I may practice bad faith with a good conscience, since this is the way I am and the way all people are. It is this failure to love, due to a fundamental defect in the capacity of a person to love, that fuels the ideology of the self-made radical individualist, whether in American business, literature, or imperial politics.

The second principle of this dialectical logic of vision is the surplus value derived from the refusal (really the inability) to mourn; this results in the experience of a rebirth of oneself as a visionary, whether prophet or entrepreneur. The death of love as a possibility repeatedly fosters the birth of the self and its "authentic" vocation as a visionary creator and not a passionate sufferer. Here is the passage from "Experience" that spells out this principle:

> When I converse with a profound mind, or if at an time being alone have good thoughts, I do not at once arrive at satisfactions, as when being thirsty, I drink water, or go to the fire, being cold: no! but I am first apprized of my vicinity to a new and excellent origin of life. By persisting to read or to think, this region gives further sign of itself, as it were in flashes of light, in sudden discoveries of its profound beauty and repose, as if the clouds that covered it parted at intervals, and showed the approaching traveler the inland mountains, with the tranquil eternal meadows spread at their base, whereon flocks graze, and shepherds pipe and dance. But every insight from this realm of thought is felt as initial, and promises a sequel. I do not make it; I arrive there, and behold what was there already. I make! O no! I clap my hands in infantine joy and amazement, before the first opening to me of this august magnificence, old with the love and homage of innumerable ages, young with the life of life, the sun bright Mecca of the desert. And what a future it opens! I feel a new heart beating with the love of a new beauty. I am ready to die out of nature, and be born again into this new yet unapproachable America I have found in the West. (169)

The difference between Emerson's vision here and Horatio Alger's is that Emerson wants to retain his innocence by passively experiencing the vision, a vision of "the Ideal journeying always before us," that he now says has become identified, largely though his own prophetic nomination, with "America." As we see, Emerson appropriates as his imaginative property—to compensate for the loss of his son-estate, perhaps—both the Elysian Fields of the Greeks and the Mecca of Islam. In spatializing cultural history imperialistically, then, Emerson demonstrates once again that he experiences reading another mind and thinking alone as the same thing. He makes what appears to be a relation into evidence of a rapacious self-identity. He then places this new version of the transcendental Ideal, which does penetrate him and provoke his lover's ardor because it is himself in another guise, in the West of America. Clearly, this West may in fact be located anywhere, as it is a place of thought, a place in thought, a conceptual and rhetorical topic that will become fully in our time what I call global America. And rather than simply saying Emerson compensates for the death of his son by refusing to mourn and then uses this surplus of libido to fund his new version of the Ideal as if giving birth to his son anew in the guise of this Ideal, I think it is more accurate to say that Emerson performs the rebirth of his self-love, more maniacally intense, in the project of "this new yet unapproachable America." The new heart he feels beating is his own. He has become his own father-mother-son, and another name for that imaginative monster would be global America.

This is the logic of vision in American literature in its purest form. Even such a sophisticated and ironical figure as Henry James feels the pull of Emerson's visionary logic. And in his early resistance he will reveal how Emerson's apparently provincial nationalistic vision underpins liberal urbane cosmopolitanism, which is also clearly indebted to European intellectual sources and visions of world literature. In a letter to Thomas Perry (1867), the young Henry James exhibits a combined Hegelian/Goethean/Emersonian confidence in being an American:

> We young Americans are . . . men of the future. I feel that my only chance for success . . . is to let all the breezes of the west blow

through me at their will. We are American born.... I look upon it as a great blessing; and I think that to be an American is an excellent preparation for culture. We have exquisite qualities as a race, and it seems to me that we are ahead of the European races in the fact that ... we can deal freely with forms of civilization not our own, can pick and choose and assimilate and in short (aesthetically etc.) claim our property wherever we find it. To have no national stamp has hitherto been a regret and a drawback, but I think it not unlikely that American writers may yet indicate that a vast intellectual fusion and synthesis of the various National tendencies of the world is the condition of the more important achievements than any we have seen.[3]

I bring in Henry James to stress that for American intellectuals of the period, the freedom of aesthetic or imaginative appropriation of (or affiliation with) other cultures and nationalities, for whatever promising purpose of would-be liberation, depends for its very conceivability upon the logic of vision articulated by Emerson. As James puts it so well, "we can deal freely with forms of civilization not our own, can pick and choose and assimilate and in short (aesthetically etc.) claim our property wherever we find it."

To be fair to James, soon enough he recognizes the foolishness of this cultural project of producing "a vast intellectual fusion and synthesis of the various National tendencies of the world" under the hegemony of "we young Americans." In an 1874 essay, "M. Turgenev," James appears to reverse himself and recognize the irreducible reality of the larger world, and its particularly inescapably worldly dimension, as a fact of struggle and not facile aesthetic appropriation. Actual experience makes for the basis of an ethics of greater consciousness and understanding:

Life is a battle.... [T]he world as it stands is no illusion, no phantasm, no evil dream of a night; we wake up to it again for ever and ever; we can neither forget it nor deny it nor dispense with it. We can welcome experience as it comes, and give it what it demands, in exchange for something which it is idle to pause to call much or little so long as it contributes to swell the volume of consciousness.

In this there is mingled pain and delight, but over the mysterious mixture there hovers a visible rule; that bids us learn to will and to seek to understand . . . .[4]

Much of James's subsequent fiction may be seen in light of this different appreciation of the world and of experience.[5]

In focusing on what Donald Pease calls "Emersonianism," I do not want to leave the impression that this logic of vision is the only one. For one brief but familiar example we can turn to William Butler Yeats, who follows Blake, if not Freud, to see a mode of vision that, while largely individual, takes a different turn than those of Emerson or James. In "*Per Amica Silentia Lunae*" (1917), the poet climbs to the waste room alone and must chew over "the bitter crust" of some remnant of his youthful vision in hopes of inspiring himself to new visions. This leads to Yeats's most famous pronouncement about the visionary process: "I shall find the dark grow luminous, the void fruitful, when I realize I have nothing, that the ringers in the tower have appointed for the hymen of my soul a passing-bell."[6] Here, the visionary logic turns back on the visionary and is internalized, producing the recognition that experience is tragically penetrating and entails inescapable loss, and that is, as Nietzsche would say, a matter of *amor fati*. It is not to be denied or compensated for by mad projects for world transformation. This is comparable to the truth event in Badiou, understood as a singular vision of a new multiple set breaking into experience. The subject of this truth event is collective and constitutes itself only via the various truth processes worked out among the members of the collective over time in the joint effort to preserve and develop fidelity to, and rational conviction about, the truth event.

To spell out why I think it is necessary to confront and critique "Emersonianism," by which I mean the logic of vision in American literature and culture as I have laid it out here, I would point to the continuing fiasco, beyond tragedy, in Iraq. The pattern is clear: the refusal to accept catastrophic loss (9/11) and internalize it, incorporating it into a more humane personal and/or cultural super-ego, so that it may act both as a check on the narcissistic drive (evidenced so clearly in the passages from Emerson discussed previously) and as a humanizing force in one's relationships with others, perfectly captures the mindset of George W. Bush and his closest advisors. The elective, preemptive military "adventure" in Iraq is precisely the discovery, yet again, of "this new yet unapproachable America," but this time as if found uncannily in some "sunbright Mecca of the desert," in an insane neo-conservative wet dream that in arrogant ignorance overlooks the realities of the region, its peoples and their histories, and indeed of the larger world generally.

In declaring this, I do not mean to suggest that this mindset is necessarily coincident with Bush's and his advisors' psychologies at every point, or even in most points. Rather, I am suggesting that via the operation of education, popular culture, and all the usual apparatus of modern U.S. culture, there is available to anyone what Blake would call a "State" that one can enter and pass through, or get stuck in and cling to for security's sake. This "State" is less a Hegelian "spirit of the age" than what Pierre Bourdieu terms a "habitus," what Foucault calls "a disciplinary practice," or what I would simply name, after its ubiquity in popular culture, "the American dream." For reasons of history, economic reality, and personal development (or lack of same), "Emersonianism" is one such "State" and in our moment the preferred "State of the State." By both exposing Emerson's logic wherever and whenever it appears in American literature and culture, and by setting forth the opposing logics, some of which I have just mentioned, we practice both a literary politics and a literary ethics that can hopefully help in time to change the educational apparatus, and through that change to some extent the media apparatus.

What I have in mind can be indicated by a passage that I will conclude, from Robert Stone's riveting memoir remembering the 1960s, *Prime Green:*

> What I will never forget [about visiting Ken Kesey, his family, and friends—the band of "merry pranksters" Stone knew so well—in Mexico in 1966] is the greening of the day at first light on the shores north of Manzanillo Bay. I imagine that color so vividly.... In the moments after dawn, before the sun had reached the peaks of the sierra, the slopes and valleys of the rain forest would explode in green light, erupting inside a silence that seemed barely to contain it. When the sun's rays spilled over the ridge, they discovered dozens of

silvery waterspouts and dissolved them into smoky rainbows. Then the silence would give way, and jungle noises rose to blue heavens. Those mornings, day after day, made nonsense of examined life, but they made everyone smile. All of us, stoned or otherwise, caught in the vortex of the dawn, would freeze in our tracks and stand to, squinting in the pain of the light, sweating, grinning. We called that light Prime Green; it was primal, primary, primo.[7]

To me, the importance of such a passage as a counterforce to the logic of vision in Emerson (and through him generally in American culture) lies not in the suggestion, following William Wordsworth, that love of nature leads inevitably to love of man, but that this vision of Prime Green is a vision of Being, of the real. Whatever its sublime dimensions, it is essentially experienced as a penetrating beauty whose force and transcendent power chastens and inspires Stone and the community of "merry pranksters" there in Mexico over forty years ago. The loss of this vision, however, inspires no violent projects of displacement and denial, of sublimity. Instead, the state of mind in this passage is one clearly of continuing joyful love. At the risk of courting sentimentality, one that Stone's austere style gently controls here, I would want such a logic of vision to supplant that which has haunted American literature and culture from Emerson's time at least to the present moment.

5

AMERICA, THE SYMPTOM

On the Post-9/11 Allegory in American Studies

AS I ELABORATE throughout *Empire Burlesque: The Fate of Critical Culture in Global America*, abjection is a technical, theoretical term and concept in Julia Kristeva's revisionary feminist post-Lacanian psychoanalysis. I will not on this occasion repeat my critical elaborations of abjection, sparing you the often-dark intricacies of mucking around in our more abstruse psychic exfoliations and excretions. I know that may spoil the fun for some of us, but instead of that course, I will take another by discussing my position on criticism with broader accessible examples to underscore my point, I hope, with more immediacy.

Strangely enough, two scenes from Arnold Schwarzenegger films, *Last Action Hero* (1993) and *True Lies* (1994), hover over my following reflections as I do so. The first scene, from *Last Action Hero*, is that of the figure of Death, from Ingmar Bergman's classic *The Seventh Seal* (1957), coming out of the film and stepping off the screen into the movie theater while the audience runs, literally, for its life. The second scene, from *True Lies*, is that of Arnold Schwarzenegger flying his jet into a skyscraper trying to rescue Jamie Lee Curtis from the Islamic terrorists who plan to fire nuclear missiles at Miami. The time of the Reagan and first Bush administrations is a fertile one for such fantasy images that return to us in the real, with a twist, sometime later, as they so clearly do on 9/11. And now to my assignment.

While I borrowed the main title of *Empire Burlesque* from a 1987 album of that same name by Bob Dylan, I coined the phrase "global America" in the book's subtitle of *The Fate of Global America*. (I took from Emerson my sense of "fate" as an ever-diminishing expression of human agency.) What did I mean by "global America"? I meant and still mean the horizon of possibility defining the present moment and its foreseeable future in the planet's human history. Within this fateful horizon, critical culture, that is, the culture of intellectuals adverse and resistant to the hegemony of any one national power, would now and hereafter, for some time to come, have to operate, for better and for worse. Global America, therefore, is a figure for the admittedly diminished prospects of criticism.

By identifying the international processes of globalization, which include the resistances to, as well as the collaborations with, my figure of global America, I am not assuming anything permanent about the actual position of the United States, whatever its military prowess has been. I recognize now, for instance, that the country has become drastically weakened geopolitically and in terms of its cultural influence, due to the foreign policy disasters of the Bush administration. Nonetheless, my view is that the global cultural stage upon which we all must play is increasingly situated as a sensational scene of self-abjection, as if simply to appear publicly requires us to perform a pole dance in the strip club of criticism, or whatever is your equivalent figure for the lowest common denominator of popular tastes. Perhaps your figure for such tastes might run to the personal blogs of would-be leading critics detailing their every daily movement?

The assessment I made when *Empire Burlesque* came out in 2003 and that I still make today is this: the prospects for criticism are not good. As I see it, the economic processes connected with globalization have reduced criticism to a broad parody of itself and its oppositional gestures, on the model of the global phenomenon apparently most suited to our benighted time: professional wrestling. As in wrestling, criticism has its latest baby faces or heroes, and its old heels or hard-core villains, the ubiquitous slogans and catchphrases, the predictable finishing maneuvers, all done under the transparent guise of one or another identity theme—the barbwire baseball bat–wielding lone cowboy, the nasty foreign menace (or heroic postcolonial victim), the sleazy ladies' man, the demented, fire-throwing maniac, the cross-dressing ass man, the femme fatale, Goth or punk, or the femme (or butch) diva, and so on. And throughout this reduced scene of criticism I tried to offer the elements of a (self-)critique and in terms that might have the potential for transforming the entire game and playing another one with different rules, however utopian that prospect seemed then (or seems now). Most of *Empire Burlesque* thus explores the emerging rules of this reduced game of globalized criticism as it developed from 1993 to 2001, attempting to bend those rules or even break open the game, by making what we do available for other, more serious critical purposes.

In the introduction to *Empire Burlesque,* I put into play the term "authentic gimmick." This term comes from the first of Mick Foley's three memoirs of his life as a professional wrestler.[1] According to Foley, the authentic gimmick is the distinguishing trait of a wrestler's performance based on some feature of his or her actual personality that his adopted persona exaggerates into an identity marker like a brand name. So while Foley (as Cactus Jack, one of his three wrestling personae) is not really from Truth or Consequences or New Mexico, nor has he served time in jail for manslaughter, his high-risk daredevil antics, like letting himself be thrown off a twenty-foot-high steel cage onto a TV announcers' table in a Hell-in-a-Cell match with the Undertaker in 1999, compose a hyperbolic performance of his aspiration to such bizarre subjectivity. These daredevil antics, in short, help largely to define his authentic gimmick. By inserting this term into the critical context of identity politics, I hoped both to make use of such a context and to burlesque it, insofar as such politics play into the representative corporate culture of global America with its too-often empty multicultural political correctness.

It was after *Empire Burlesque* appeared in early 2003 (but composed nearly two years before) that I began studying closely the philosophy of Alain Badiou. I came to his work via my reading of Jacques Lacan and his commentators and was moved by the event of 9/11 to examine his thinking. The apparently "impossible" had happened—the United States had been attacked at home, right in the symbolic heart of its financial and cultural modernity—and that "impossibility" made me feel that the prospects of criticism had to be projected upon the basis not of the merely possible, but upon that of the "impossible" too. What captured me in Badiou was his theory of truth, which is all about the "impossible" infinite coming to pass in and as authentic history.

The real theoretical advantage of Badiou lies precisely in his position on truth. Truth, for him, is not a matter of correspondence between a statement and a state of affairs, such as "it is raining," when it is; nor is it a matter of the internal coherence of statements made about something, such as the axiomatic definitions of geometric figures; nor is truth, as it is for Nietzsche, a matter of the lie or fiction we have forgotten or never admitted to ourselves is a lie or a fiction, such as the myriad of dead metaphors in language or the love we feel for another but have never fully acted on. As for Heidegger, so for Badiou: truth is an event. But unlike Heidegger, who declares that truth is the unveiling of Being that appropriates us via the poet's creative saying or the philosopher's formative thinking, Badiou describes truth as an event subtracted from being, which for him is the indifferent infinities of multiples upon multiples that make up mathematics. For Badiou, mathematics alone is the bleak ontology of being; so truth, in this unusual context, is then the explosive event of the void haunting being suddenly, unexpectedly, and impossibly manifesting itself as a contingent hole in established knowledge. The sequences of youth revolts all around the world in 1968—in France, in Czechoslovakia, in China, in the United States, etc.—are examples of the truth event.

In order to understand even better what Badiou means by the truth event, we have to focus on how human beings experience existence in terms of situations. A situation, as we have seen, is the presentation of Being within the human horizon. A situation therefore presents a multiple of elements composing a set. Each set of elements has a state of knowledge, what Badiou calls its "encyclopedia," which inventories the set's members. A set is composed of those elements *belonging* to the set and those fully *included* as *members* of the set. To be included as a member of a set is to be *a part incorporated into a subset of the set, and so to be counted officially.* To belong to a set just means that the elements in question have been presented by the situation but not integrated by the count into the set as a represented

CHAPTER 5 | AMERICA, THE SYMPTOM

subset. The state of the situation refers to the operation of counting as members all those elements that count for that state based on the encyclopedia of knowledge for that situation. This vicious circle of knowledge explains why truth must appear as the impossible interruption of all established logics. Thus, what a situation presents and what is represented as the situation by the state are never the same thing.

Such a gap between presentation and representation in any situation is its constitutive void. The state of the situation then generates many names from the established encyclopedia of knowledge to cover over this void. These are contradictory or antagonistic names, whose lack of determinate meaning continues to haunt the situation with semantic and ontological instability. (The original "three-fifths of a man count" in the Constitution that defined the slave is a good case in point.) The truth event happens when the void founding the situation and inadequately covered over by organized knowledge and its conventional names is experienced by those living on the void's edge—I will call them "the purely abject"—as incommensurate with any and all of these official names. It is then that the void can irrupt into the situation through the purely abject's newly self-empowered subjective agency for their naming the void in their own terms, thereby exposing the situation to the conflict between presented and represented elements that the state has tried to cover up and suppress. The truth event is always fleeting and often fragile, even if it inspires impressive sequences of fidelity to it. The Civil War and the civil rights movement are instances of this explosive truth event and its consequent sequences of fidelity that punch holes in the state of current knowledge for the situations of their respective times.

In this light, is 9/11, for the perpetrators, a truth event? According to Badiou, it is not.[2] This is because a truth event always has as a consequence a truth procedure attached to it, that is, a declaration bearing witness to the truth of the event as such, and although the Bush administration attributed 9/11 to Osama Bin Laden and his followers, no one formally took responsibility for the event in a statement, which for Badiou is essential to any truth procedure following a truth event. Otherwise, what appears as the irruption of the truth event is actually just the latest form of nihilism. Whether the truth event occurs in politics, art, science, or love—the four domains of

85

truth that philosophy coordinates and clarifies critically—the consequent truth procedure incorporates a discourse of witnessing that thereby defines the existence of the subject of that truth.

The best example of this relationship between truth event and truth procedure and statement is, according to Badiou, Saint Paul, because Paul's discourse of sacred mystery dispenses, in one fell stroke, with the discourses of Jewish law and classical philosophy, without resorting to a purely mystical discourse.[3] But there are other examples Badiou repeatedly deploys, including the Russian Revolution and Vladimir Lenin's writings (politics), the invention of symphonic musical form and its aesthetics or Arnold Schoenberg's twelve-tone scale (art), the theories of special and general relativity (science), and the discovery and revision of psychoanalysis in Freud and Lacan (love). Given Badiou's requirements, for those who carried it out but remained silent as death about their reasons for it, 9/11 cannot be a truth event. But can it be one for "us," its sufferers; that is, for those of us who have borne its effects and testify to them? Are we already, or can we yet make up, the post-9/11 American subject, and if so, will that make a difference in what we mean by "American" and also what we mean by criticism? Is there a discernible truth of the 9/11 event for all its victims, or not?

An admittedly evident way to think about 9/11 is that it brings home to Americans that ours is not an exceptional nation, ordained by history or providence, to act in the world apparently with perpetual immunity, thanks also in part to our geographic protection by two oceans. Ours, in the words of John Ashbery's title to his latest book of poems, is "a worldly country," not a virgin land impervious to what the rest of the world is open to all the time.[4] Neither a shining city on the hill nor a legendary Byzantium, America is both of and in the world, for better and for worse. As such, the post-9/11 global America is a symptom of the state of the world system. To understand more fully what I mean by this formulation, we must take a digression into Lacan's theory of the symptom.

In *Seminar 23: Le Sinthome,* Lacan gives his pithiest definition of the drive. It is "the echo in the body of the fact of speech" ("c'est l'écho dans le corps du fait qu'il y à un dire").[5] A drive arises then in the act of speaking. It inhabits the body as a repeated echoing, a constant force of reverberation, moving ceaselessly (as long as it can) into an open-ended future within the matrix of the symbolic order and the narcissistic mirages of the imaginary. As such, the drive, in the act of a saying, is a rendering of the real, a writing, an inscription of the voice, in and upon the self-invaginating surface of the body. The drive does not ever not write, as Lacan reminds us, rehearsing that primal saying marking the subject of the signifier. The drive is a writing of the letter that in principle is endless, infinite, carrying the eternity or immortality effect, like the Longinian sublime. This infinite writing is a visionary figuration of the real simultaneously transcending and disclosing the limits of symbolic representation. Such a sublime writing is located in an entirely self-referential scene of instruction, an antimimetic dramatic act of saying—a pure performance of the real. The symptom of this drive-propelled inscription, an echo of the necessary fiction of a primal saying, is thus inherently theatrical and figurative, productive of a theatre of trope, and, in its formal embodiment, capable of being turned to use by the artist as an aesthetic support of his or her psyche, as Lacan shows in James Joyce's case. The symptom in Joyce, now revised into *le sinthome* by the art of the letter, becomes a supplemental structure suturing the wobbly Borromean knot of the three registers of the real, the Symbolic, and the Imaginary. That is, the power of revisionary naming transforms the painful compromise formation of the symptom into the new structural principle of jouissance that Lacan christens *le sinthome*.

I want to suggest that global America after 9/11 has become just such a symptom/*sinthome* dyad. Insofar as we publicly and repeatedly disavow all the evidence demonstrating the fiction of American exceptionalism, we will see returning to us in the real of world system the symptomatic, unconscious truth of our situation. But insofar as we avow this symptom of global America, we can make use of this figure sinthomatically to tie together our traumatically disarranged psychic agencies (after 9/11) into a new supplementary pattern open to the truth of the U.S. position in the world. In light of this double-edged possibility, we can read anew older texts by American writers, as well as appreciate new texts in unpredictable ways.

Although set in England, "The Beast in the Jungle" (1904) by Henry James can be and has been read as expressing James's sense of his father's fateful sense of anticlimax.[6] Certainly, the haunting of its male protagonist by the visionary figure of his own creation, "the beast in the jungle," as symbolic of his *sui generis* destiny, recalls both the author of the tale's feeling of distinction and, even more so perhaps, Henry James Senior's famous scene of "vastation," when he was literally haunted by a monstrous hallucination for days and nights on end during his son and namesake's early childhood. Moreover, I would suggest that the idea of infinite exceptional promise infinitely deferred in its realization is a theme memorably explored in Emerson's classic essay "Experience" (1844). In short, James in this tale has sounded an American and personal theme, regardless of the locale of the setting.

"The Beast in the Jungle" is a tale about a man whose symptom, ironically enough, is that he is exceptionally unmarked by any symptom. That is to say, John Marcher passes for the perfectly normal man, even as he manifests narcissism so terrible in its isolating deception that he is totally unaware of its existence, and other people exist for him only insofar as they serve his interests. He is obsessed with the idea that his unmarked status is a sign that he will have been marked before he dies by some distinction so unexpected and unprecedented that, like Freud's psychotic jurist Schreber, he awaits its advent with a meticulous watching for the tiniest sign of such exceptional election. Joined in this curious adventure by May Bartram, Marcher passes the better part of his life in her company, in which they share together his evident folly. So intimate do they appear to be that even Marcher recognizes that she often seems to be looking with him through the public mask that he wears, his gaze and hers being, at such times, as if one. Despite such apparent intimacy, however, when on the eve of her death, Marcher grills May relentlessly about what it is she now seems to know about his fate, he fails to see in the sick woman's gestures all the obvious signs of her love. She then collapses back into her chair from this climactic effort to illuminate Marcher as to his fate of being incapable of true love. What they have called "the beast in the jungle" of his fanciful ever-coming distinction is now confirmed as being, ironically enough, that he is, of all his generation, the only one to whom nothing significant will have happened, for he will remain unmarked by and impervious to any passion. Marcher fails again to realize this awful truth now, which the reader sees all too vividly.

All that Marcher knows is that after her imminent death he will be left alone to his own devices.

Once May does die, he goes global, circling the globe in a desperate attempt to fill up his life. On his return, however, he begins frequenting the cemetery, this "garden of death," as he calls it, where she lies buried, and this ritual comes to replace his visits to her in life (309). One day he has an uncanny vision of his present self walking arm in arm with his younger self, around the gravesite that May's spirit establishes as the fixed point, with her spectral gaze confirming the continuous identity of Marcher's two selves:

> [H]e seemed to wander through the old years with his hand in the arm of a companion who was, in the most extraordinary manner, his other, his younger self; and to wander, which was more extraordinary yet, round and round a third presence—not wandering she, but stationary, still, whose eyes, turning with his revolution, never ceased to follow him, and whose seat was his point, so to speak, of orientation. Thus in short he settled to live—feeding only on the sense that he once had lived, and dependent on it not only for a support but for an identity. (309)

Marcher's narcissism stages this imaginary tableau perfectly if insensitively at the gravesite, attempting thereby to evade the reality of death it ritually memorializes. Because the figure of the beast in the jungle has repeatedly stitched together Marcher's psyche and his relationship with May, having been his avowed symptom and symbol, "muse" and "demon" are apparently equated by this tableau.

The beast itself does at last make its climactic appearance at the tale's end. After seeing the passion of loss in the face of another man who comes to visit his recently deceased wife, Marcher realizes what is missing from his response to May and to his life generally: the ravages of any true passion. Trying desperately to turn this very insight itself into a real passion, the attempt sickens him virtually at once, and he collapses, losing his focus on anything other than the state of his own feelings. As he collapses onto the gravestone, however, he glimpses, with full awareness, just before he turns to hide his eyes in his arms again, the figure of the beast in the jungle spring at last:

> The horror of waking—this was knowledge, knowledge under the breath of which the very tears in his eyes seemed to freeze. Through them, none the less, he tried to fix it and hold it; he kept it there before him so that he might feel the pain. That at least, belated and bitter had something of the taste of life. But the bitterness suddenly sickened him, and it was as if, horribly, he saw, in the truth, in the cruelty of his image, what had been appointed and done. He saw the Jungle of his life and saw the lurking Beast; then, while he looked, perceived it, as by a stir of the air, rise, huge and hideous, for the leap that was to settle him. His eyes darkened—it was close; and, instinctively turning, in his hallucination, to avoid it, he flung himself, on his face, on the tomb. (312)

The precision of thrust and hesitation in this dramatic prose raises this scene of instruction to the level of visionary poetry.

"The Beast in the Jungle" concludes with this ironic apocalypse of its pathetic protagonist, whose final plight provides the text in which he persists with *le sinthome* tying together the imaginary, symbolic, and real registers of its subjective formation. Neither a symbol of any one character or idea, as May might be for Marcher, nor a fantasy of the author, however much its vehicle is Marcher's hallucination, this figure of the beast in the jungle springing upon him through the air performs the allegory of any possible reading of the text it formally holds both together and open. "The beast in the jungle" is James's sublime figure for the vision of modern literature that overcomes the subject not strong enough to accede to its terrifyingly infinite drive of the real.

As we can see even at the end here, what for the character functions as a symptom of fatal waste can become for the critical reader the sublime basis of the healing *sinthome*. Moreover, what the reader now sees, much as May previously saw, comes through the character's eyes, and as we see the beast in the jungle as well as the character's fate, we also see then as the author does, that it hovers upon the air generally, returning from its psychic hideout to the real of the situation the tale establishes, a phantasm of personal apocalypse once shared by two (Marcher and May) and, as a cautionary tale, presented now to all.

As we have seen, a strong model in American literature for any such apocalyptic (self-)illumination is the passage in Emerson's "Experience" where he observes "the mode of our illumination" by the visionary moment.[7] Like the truth event, this moment comes to us without calculation, in pure contingency, even as it tells of the truth that inhabits our experience, however broken, bereaved, or isolated. Here is the key passage when, for Emerson, symptom becomes *sinthome*, as a dreaded fate becomes, for him in the central passage of his "Experience," a beloved joy—but at a tragic cost: "I feel a new heart beating with the love of the new beauty. I am ready to die out of nature, and be born again into this new yet unapproachable America I have found in the West" (262).

Just as the beast in the jungle springing into the air in James's tale initiates the would-be-exceptional Marcher at last into the common world of human experience, so too does 9/11, truly experienced, serve to do so for any latter-day exceptionalist American Marchers in our global world. Thus, Emerson provides us with the direction to go from here, to transform our trauma into a creative occasion of imaginative rebirth, by reading, listening, thinking, rather than rashly acting and ignoring or disavowing our feelings and those of others. For us, following Emerson's lead here, we may give birth to ourselves at last (or, perhaps, once again), provided we, unlike him, do not sacrifice the power to love to the quest for reason.

It is in this context that I want to conclude by discussing the significance of Jonathan Lear's *Radical Hope: Ethics in the Face of Cultural Devastation*.[8] Although 9/11 is never specifically mentioned, we can infer its absent "beast-in-jungle" phantasmal presence symptomatically haunting such remarks as the following, from the opening: "We live in a time of a heightened sense that civilizations are themselves vulnerable. Events around the world—terrorist attacks, violent social upheavals, and natural catastrophes—have left us with an uncanny sense of menace" (7). Ironically, though, among academic professionals, Lear's book has been read either in terms of identity politics or as a purely liberal cautionary tale about how we in the West should understand those civilizations our capitalist modernity threatens in so many ways. However, when I taught this book to my students at Temple University in a senior English major capstone seminar ("D. H. Lawrence's 'America'"), they read the book almost entirely for how it spoke to their fears inspired by 9/11. I find this split in response telling, as I will try to demonstrate.

Lear's *Radical Hope* tells the story of the Crow Indian Chief, Plenty Coups, and his practical understanding of and response to his people being forced onto the reservation and having to give up their way of life as hunters and warriors for the settled life of farmers. Something Plenty Coups said at the end of his life, that after the buffalo were mostly wiped out and he and his people were forcibly confined to the reservation, "after this nothing happened," provides the text for Lear to interpret (2). The cultural devastation or culture death that the Crow experienced centers on their symbolic act of planting the coup stick. This is a wooden spear decorated with feathers and scalps used to mark the boundary between the territory of the Crow hunters and that of any rival for that territory. Because the Crow people's entire way of life, for all the tribe's members, is defined by such comparatively elementary ritualistic acts, once they are on the reservation, confined to a farming life, planting the coup stick for them can no longer mean anything; it is as if their lives have come to an end, not only psychologically but ontologically. That is, once the historically defined schemas that form their sense of space and time, inform their imagination, and pervade their recognition of the world have been abolished, the Crow are without anchoring concepts, principles, and values to make even rudimentary sense of experience. They are adrift, at sea, like the undead aboard some ghost ship.

Lear goes on to argue that Plenty Coups, by making use of the resources of his tradition, was able to lead his people to survival, albeit in diminished circumstances, but to survival nonetheless. Unlike Sitting Bull, whose courage takes the form of rashness in his radical opposition to the U.S. government and military, or the many Indian scouts whose courage in performing their duties was in the service of collaboration to ensure their own personal survival, Plenty Coups' courage sought primarily to serve his people's survival on their own land. (Lear develops this Aristotelian golden mean schema of virtue to generalize Plenty Coups' example beyond the specific or "thick" terms of his life into a broader, "thinner" concept that, he hopes, can be put to many uses in often quite different contexts.)

Specifically, what Plenty Coups does is to make use of his tradition's myth of the "Chickadee," the little bird that is a trickster figure in Crow storytelling. Plenty Coups goes into the woods and has a dream-vision, in which this bird instructs him to observe, listen, and learn enough of the ways of others to allow Plenty Coups to serve as a chief who can lead his people to survive, admittedly in reduced circumstances, but at least with a somewhat renewed form of their culture. "Radical hope" is then the courage to act in the face of culture death amid all the persistent uncertainty of not even being able to envisage the full shape of the good such hope may help to bring about. Like Keatsian "negative capability" for the poet, but even more dire and indeterminate, radical hope can empower a person or a people and their culture to live on, anew.

The professional response to the book has seemed odd to me. Either, as in the humanities reading group at Temple, academics such as Lewis Gordon (Philosophy), Rebecca Alpert (Religion/Women's Studies), and Steve Newman (English) read it simply in accord with the one-dimensional themes of their own identity politics as a provincial "bad" liberal white man's self-serving racialist manifesto; or, as in Charles Taylor's following remarks from his review essay for *The New York Review of Books,* the book comes off as a worldly "good" liberal's cautionary tale for the West:[9]

> What do I take away from this short, illuminating book? My own version of radical hope applied to very different circumstances. Like the version Lear attributes to the Crow, this starts with a devastating realization: that the emergence of a world civilization, highly unified economically, politically, and in communication, has exacted, and will go on exacting, a tremendous human cost in the death or near death of cultures. And this will be made worse because those who dominate modern civilization have trouble grasping what the costs involve. (24)

Taylor has already stipulated that our modern civilization is far different from the Crow culture, in terms of what constitutes the fund of basic elements of concepts and principles defining the respective peoples. We are "richer" in that respect, with more resources to draw on than simply planting the coup stick. But we are richer, according to Taylor, also in terms of the comparative flexibility of self-identity our civilization possesses and endorses, as opposed to that of the strictly hunter-warrior culture of the Crow. In fact, we now encourage young people to assume the possibility of having to develop many different subjectivities over their lifetime, for the economy will require them to perform many jobs in the future.

In this "liberal" differential context, here is the rest of Taylor's version of radical hope:

> [My own radical] hope comes from Lear's account of Crow society: that human beings can find the resources to come back from a virtual dead end, and invent a new way of life in some creative continuity with the one that has been condemned, as the Crow did in embracing settled agriculture. The hope is "radical," because it is virtually impossible to say beforehand what the hope of this new kind of life will be. This has to emerge in specific new forms, drawing on the particular cultural resources of each society. There is no general formula, except utterly empty, formal ones, like: "find a novel solution from within your own traditions." The notion that there could be a how-to manual for this kind of creative initiative is close to absurd. In spite of that, a powerful stream of thought and policy in our society persists in thinking in such hortatory ways. There is, for example, the notion that so-called experts can be dispatched to teach societies that have been living for centuries under authoritarian rule how to become democracies. Some even think that it's obvious how to do this—just hold elections. All people, we are told, desire "freedom"; we just have to remove the bad guys who are stopping them from having it. The naïve, destructive rhetoric of the Bush administration is an extreme case, but many less crude versions of the same idea underpin Western policies of development. . . . This is what makes Lear's well-written and philosophically sophisticated book so valuable. As a story of courage and moral imagination, it is very powerful and moving. But it also offers the kind of insights that would-be builders of "new world order" desperately need. (26)

Well, I don't know what I find worse: my professional colleagues at Temple reading Lear's book habitually in terms of their oppositional identity themes; or Taylor reading it patronizingly as a liberal cautionary tale for President Bush and his neoconservative policy makers and executors eventually to have fathomed and gotten on board with.

I think I prefer instead what my twenty-two- or twenty-three-year-old students, from very diverse "global" backgrounds, had to say. Whether they referred to 9/11 in detail or some other manmade or natural catastrophe as they read the story of Plenty Coups and the Crow people, they saw that story as continuous with their own American contexts and identities now and into their new, yet ever radically unknown, futures. That is, they saw *their* cultural devastation (that of the Crow people) as a potentially prophetic version of *our* (U.S.) "impossible" truth event, as signaled and announced by 9/11. My students were reading Lear, in other words, like the "Chickadee." 9/11 had opened up a symptomatic hole in their conventional knowledge so that they could experience the truth event of cultural devastation in its most terrible, because universalizable, infinitude.

Given global America's real situation we all, too, should be unceasingly hearing Death hovering in the mid-air of our lives, even as we recall, perhaps, among other things, one of Wallace Stevens's most resourceful late poems about such creative responsiveness, "Large Red Man Reading" (1947), written at the dawning of the atomic age and in the face of his recent diagnosis of the cancer that would kill him.[10]

> There were ghosts that returned to earth to hear his phrases,
> As he sat there reading, aloud, the great blue tabulae.
> They were those from the wilderness of stars that had expected
>   more.
>
> There were those that returned to hear him from the poem of life,
> Of the pans above the stove, the pots on the table, the tulips
>   among them.
> They were those that would have wept to step barefoot into reality,
>
> That would have wept and been happy, have shivered in the frost
> And cried out to feel it again, have run fingers over leaves
> And against the most coiled thorn, have seized on what was ugly
>
> And laughed, as he sat there reading, from out of the purple tabulae,

The outlines of being and its expressing, the syllables of its law:
Poesis, poesis, the literal characters, the vatic lines,

Which in those ears and in those thin, those spended hearts,
Took on color, took on shape and the size of things as they are
And spoke the feeling for them, which was what they had lacked.
(423–24)

To be completely fair to Stevens, I must add in conclusion that no one knows for sure what he meant by "Large Red Man Reading." It could be, of course, the once common epithet for a Native American or the Indian; but it could also be one of his most favorite and central figures, that of the solar wheel, a Whitman-like celestial vagabond-clown here reading the auguries of the sky and future fates, as the day fades from blue to purple tabulae. This would fit with the volume this poem appears in, *The Auroras of Autumn* (1947). But the figure could also be, as one of his letters suggest, how he felt he must have looked during a reading at the front of the room, as the Princeton audience begin to leave, looking back at him as his now hoarse voice somehow grew a bit louder and hastier. In any event, this cosmic image of the prophetic reader just may be his (and now our) most appropriate critical figure for the "little chickadee" of Chief Plenty Coups.[11]

6

OUR WORLDLY APOCALYPSE

Literature and Everyday Life

I WILL SELECT for my point of departure a quotation from "The Brown Stocking," the famous last chapter on Virginia Woolf, in *Mimesis,* Erich Auerbach's magisterial study of the history of representation in Western literature. This chapter fulfills, figuratively speaking, with a gentle irony the promise of his even more famous opening chapter on Homer, "Odysseus' Scar":

> What takes place here in Virginia Woolf's novel [*To the Lighthouse*] is precisely what was attempted everywhere in the works of this kind ... that is, to put the emphasis on the random occurrence, to exploit it not in the service of a planned continuity of action but in itself. And in the process something new and elemental appeared: nothing less than the wealth of reality and depth of life in every moment to which we surrender ourselves without prejudice. To be sure, what happens in that moment—be it outer or inner processes—concerns in a very personal way the individuals who live in it, but it also (and for that very reason) concerns the elementary things which men in general have in common. It is precisely the random moment which is comparatively independent of the controversial and unstable orders over which men fight and despair; it passes unaffected by them, as daily life. The more it is exploited, the more

the elementary things which our lives have in common come to light. The more numerous, varied and simple the people appear as subject of such random moments, the more effectively must what they have in common shine forth. In this unprejudiced and exploratory type of representation we cannot but see to what an extent—below the surface conflicts—the differences between men's ways of life and forms of thought have already lessened. (552)[1]

Auerbach goes on to worry that what he judges to be a relatively common event, this random moment of imaginative insight, this new universal of everyday life that is revealed by modern literature's worldly realism and that stands beyond or apart (to some degree) from the political wars and conflicts of the times—that this practice of everyday life will likely become, in its turn, subject to the great simplification of a reductive regime of mass consumer culture. This will be, for Auerbach, writing at the end of World War II, either an American or a Stalinist global order—an order to replace those other totalitarian ones just destroyed. However rueful his—and our—awakening to this baleful historical prospect may be, Auerbach has progressively revealed in *Mimesis* this worldly apocalypse of everyday life, as I will call it.

This literary vision is fully realized, for Auerbach, in *To the Lighthouse*'s Mrs. Ramsay sewing her son James's brown stocking, with her unguarded expression making her face appear to be the most beautiful and the saddest face anyone has ever seen. It stands in counterpoint to Odysseus's faithful maidservant recognizing her master by the manly scar he obtained from the noble hunt. And Auerbach argues that this imaginative representation of the everyday world has progressively become (naturally with setbacks along the way) the subject of literature from Homer to Woolf. Certainly, this ironically stated "Hebraic" vision of Auerbach's immediately discloses to us its romantic, Hegelian, Vichian, and generally Enlightenment provenance. My point in jumping off from this vision is not to elaborate on all its features or to perform a critical genealogy. Nor is it to demonstrate self-contradicting beginnings and take the legs out from under Auerbach's delicately made argument. Rather, my point is to offer a viable and sturdy rationale for the future of English studies, which for me, at this time, means the future of literary studies.

Much work has been done on the idea of "everyday life." One of the best recent books on the subject is Michael Sheringham's *Everyday Life: Theories and Practices from Surrealism to the Present*.[2] And we know or have heard of the names of everyday life's influential and diverse thinkers, such as Erving Goffman, Michel de Certeau, and perhaps even such names as Georges Perec and Eric Santner. Of the more famous and influential names, such as Charles Baudelaire, Sigmund Freud, and Martin Heidegger, we have heard, perhaps, overmuch. But I prefer on this occasion to stick with Auerbach's formulation of everyday life, given previously, with its emphasis on the fugitive or contingent moment of individual imaginative perception, grounded in the worldly reality of a people as they live their daily lives: "It is precisely the random moment which is comparatively independent of the controversial and unstable orders over which men fight and despair; it passes unaffected by them, as daily life" (552).

Auerbach's formulation of this event of the random moment in *Mimesis* can be read as an aesthetic moment, a piece of bourgeois ideology, or even a postmodern sublimity, *avant le letter*. Given my immersion in Alain Badiou's work, I could assimilate Auerbach's random moment to Badiou's theory of the truth event. But, along with Auerbach's best commentators, Edward W. Said and Paul A. Bové, I prefer not to make such moves of assimilation, finding greater critical virtue in the more open-ended turns of phrase in Auerbach's well-informed but sinuously articulate and qualifying prose. The indelible details of imaginative life arise in their sharp lucidity in the still-warm ground of such essayistic creation.

Similarly, but with an even keener edge, a long paragraph from the middle of John Cheever's great novel about prison life, *Falconer*, provides me with a surprisingly detailed and even mundane representation of the basic situation of the modern subject that literature—as the pleasurable performance of critical judgment—addresses:

> Farragut found his sense of time and space somewhat imperiled. He owned a watch and a calendar and his surroundings had never been so easily catalogued, but he had never faced with such deep apprehension the fact that he did not know where he was. He was at the head of a slalom trail, he was waiting for the train, he was waking after a bad drug trip in a hotel in New Mexico. "Hey

> Tiny," he would shout [to the guard], "where am I?" Tiny understood. "Falconer Prison," he would say. "You killed your brother." "Thanks, Tiny." So, on the strength of Tiny's voice, the bare facts would return. In order to lessen this troubling sense of otherness, he remembered that he had experienced this [profound disorientation] in the street as well. The sense of being simultaneously in two or three places at the same instant was something he had known beyond the walls. He remembered standing in an air-conditioned office on a sunny day while he seemed, at the same time, to be standing in a shabby farmhouse at the beginning of a blizzard. He could, standing in a highly disinfected office, catch the smell of a woodbox and catalogue his legitimate concerns about tire chains, snowplows and supplies of groceries, fuel and liquor—everything that concerns a man in a remote house at the beginning of a tempest. This was a memory, of course, seizing someplace in the present, but why should he, in an antiseptic room in midsummer, have unwillingly received such a memory? He tried to track it down on the evidence of smell. A wooden match burning in an ashtray might have provoked the memory. (105–6)[3]

What makes this experience of radical dissociation so disturbing for Farragut is that the temporal and spatial dissemination is more dispersed in this internal exile of Falconer Prison, and the power of the sensuous image even greater, than they were for "Marcel" in Proust's *In Search of Lost Time*. "[Farragut] had been skeptical about his sensual responsiveness ever since he had, while watching the approach of thunderstorm, been disconcerted by a wet and implacable erection" (106).

Nonetheless, Cheever goes on to note, Farragut feels he must explain this radical dissociation, or at least tie himself down to the bare coordinates of the present moment, in order to resist successfully becoming dispersed into the involuntary memory—images of his past that he has a hard time distinguishing from such facts.

> If he could explain this duality by the smoke of a burning match, he could not explain that the vividness of his farmhouse memory deeply challenged the reality of the office where he stood. To weaken and dispel the unwanted memory, he forced his mind beyond the office,

which was indeed artificial, to the incontestable fact that it was the nineteenth of July, the temperature outside was ninety-two, the time was three-eighteen and he had eaten for lunch scallops or cod cheeks with sweet tartar sauce, sour fried potatoes, salad, half a roll with butter, ice cream and coffee. Armed with these indisputable details, he seemed to scourge the farmhouse memory as one opens doors and windows to get the smoke out of a room. He was successful at establishing the reality of the office and while he was not truly uneasy about the experience, it had very definitely raised a question for which he had no information at all. (106)

What Cheever, via his protagonist Farragut, registers is that Auerbach's worry about the great unification and simplification of everyday life, under the regime of consumer or mass culture, did not work out quite the way he anxiously foresaw. The great unification and simplification remain specters of the failure of homogenizing processes of globalizing modern culture.

These failures are the built-in inefficiencies of any process of assimilation, but at least some of them result from personal and group resistances—political, social, racial, sexual, and so on—which are connected to what, for purposes of brevity, I will allude to here as "the counter-culture." Finally, and most worrisome of all, globalization depends, indeed thrives, on such an amalgam of inertial and differentiating processes for its successful operation. Cheever's own belated, painful coming out, which the novel *Falconer* partially realizes, can readily serve as one connection to these mixed effects of the radical upheavals of the 1960s and early 1970s.

In this complicated light cast by my Auerbach and Cheever examples, we can see that literature is clearly related to the great unification, simplification, and differentiation processes of global consumer culture, which the current American imperial order attempts to supervise and discipline; and just as clearly, literature is also related to the many resistances to these very processes. Literature apocalyptically discloses, demonstrates, dramatizes, and yet also composes the spatially and temporally dispersed subject of everyday life. Ironically enough, then, literature, with its imaginative visions of the random moment or event, brings out of the background and into the foreground "the incontestable details" of that life, which, as Henry James famously put it, "cannot not be known." As Auerbach remarks, such details constitute "the process of formulation and interpretation whose subject matter is our own self" (549). And as Auerbach, anticipating Cheever, puts it, this subject is not part of a totally coherent order, though in part of the world it certainly is, because, in Said's words, glossing Auerbach, there is "not one order and one interpretation, but many, which may either be those of different persons or of the same person at different times; so that overlapping, complementing and contradicting yield something that we might call a synthesized cosmic view or at least a challenge to the reader's will to interpretive synthesis" (549).

I take this challenging "cosmic view" to be the summary yet never total vision of a faithfully provisional "last" critical judgment about a text and its world that a community of different readers, or the different readings of one person, make up out of the fragmentary yet ever reverberating passages of our lives as (self-)readers. The future of English studies, of literary studies, for me, is continually learning and in my turn bearing witness to the incontestable details of this synthesized cosmic view, which is standing as a challenge to any reader's will to that total order of final "interpretive synthesis," which would as such mirror the containing order of "global America."

"LIFE ENGLOBED": ON THE AMERICAN SUBJECT

The following lines occur near the end of the first section of John Ashbery's poem "Self-Portrait in a Convex Mirror," and demonstrate, I believe, the fierce resistances to all such reflective totalities:[4]

> And just as there are no words for the surface, that is,
> No words to say what it really is, that it is not
> Superficial but a visible core, then there is
> No way out of the problem of pathos vs. experience (70)

These lines recall from earlier in the first section the more celebrated, sublimely put, declaration of the problem:

> This is what the portrait says . . .
> There is in that gaze [of Parmiginano] a combination
> Of tenderness, amusement and regret, so powerful
> In its restraint that one cannot look for long.
> The secret is too plain. The pity of it smarts,
> Makes hot tears spurt: that the soul is not a soul,
> Has no secret, is small, and it fits
> Its hollow perfectly: its room, our moment of attention . . .
> It is life englobed. (69)

In glossing these lines, I will be treading a path made by Harold Bloom and Lee Edelman in their excellent readings of Ashbery's masterpiece. In addition, many other critics over the years have shaped my general appreciation for Ashbery's artistry of self, including and especially Charles Altieri, whose latest book, *The Art of American Poetry: Modernism and After,* continues brilliantly to contribute to my understanding of Ashbery.[5]

When I read the stark, prosy formulation, "the problem of pathos vs. experience," the ultimate reference for me is not Wallace Stevens from his discussion of the self in "The Man with the Blue Guitar," nor one of Walt Whitman's innumerable discussions from "Song of Myself," but Ralph Waldo Emerson's two deliberately separated but still dialectically interrelated paragraphs from "Experience" (1844).[6] My license for such a leap comes from Ashbery himself in his poem, as he reminds himself and us that "no part / Remains that is surely you" (71).

The first of these Emersonian paragraphs testifies to the essentially superficial nature of all our experiences. Although we might willingly "even pay the costly price of sons and lovers," should that give us purchase on "the reality" of our experience, not even the loss of his son, his namesake, introduces Emerson into such passionate grief. Emerson discovers and confesses a preternatural lack of contact between subject and object, subject and other subject. While scientific analogies clarify, no amount of poetic thinking can reduce it to his understanding:

> People grieve and bemoan themselves, but it is not half so bad with them as they say. There are moods in which we court suffering, in

the hope that here, at least, we shall find reality, sharp peaks and edges of truth. But it turns out to be scene-painting and counterfeit. The only thing grief has taught me, is to know how shallow it is. That, like all the rest, plays about the surface, and never introduces me into the reality, for contact with which, we would even pay the costly price of sons and lovers. Was it Boscovitch who found out that bodies never come in contact? Well, souls never touch their objects. And innavigable sea washes silent waves between us and the things we aim at and converse with. Grief will makes us idealists. In the death of my son, now more than two years ago I seem to have a beautiful estate,—no more. I cannot get it nearer to me. If tomorrow I should be informed of the bankruptcy of my principle debtors, the loss of my property would be a great inconvenience to me, perhaps, for many years; but it would leave me as it found me,—neither better nor worse. So it is with this calamity: it does not touch me: something which I fancied was a part of me, which could not be torn away without tearing me, nor enlarged without enriching me, falls off from me, and leaves no scar. (422)

As we have seen, Emerson is not testifying here to the pathos of trauma and mourning; rather he is saying that in the death of his son, in that death of love, he thought he might have found that previously missing depth of feeling, of loss, of passion. While he hoped to have been in contact with a piercing reality, what has instead been confirmed for him is the experience of his essential separateness, as Pater would say, "the impenetrable wall of personality" surrounding him. I believe that Emerson is living, as Ashbery puts it, à la Parmigianino's and his own self-portrait, a "Life englobed." Such a life bears witness to a small soul whose secret is that its hollow holds no authentic soul at all, but only "our moment of attention" on its own substantially self-reflexive motion. Like Samuel Beckett's aural self-portraitist, Krapp, that pure drive motion can be reduced to a delight in the tastiness of a single, symptomatic word, such as "spool."

However that may be, when we read this paragraph from Emerson not in isolation but in concert with the later paragraph from "Experience" in which our hero discovers "the new yet unapproachable America . . . in the West," we find, as Stanley Cavell has beautifully written, a new founding of the nation.⁷ This second founding is a definition of America as both the space or place or scene of self-creation and the subject so created, whether that scene and self are actually "found in the West" of North America or not. I stress this point because the American subject of my title living its "life englobed" is in fact now a global subject. It is that subject whose power of suffering may not constitute a passion but whose experience of the world, precisely because of its superficiality, is always at the ready when "the moment of our attention" pauses in its perpetually self-renewing postures of reflection.

I would like also to cite the second of those two Emersonian paragraphs that I think Ashbery is commenting on in "Self-Portrait in a Convex Mirror." After reminding us, via another scientific analogy (from Sir Everard Home's work on the growth in the womb of the embryo) that "life has no memory" and does not follow a linear march of progress, Emerson suggests that "life" develops simultaneously from many points, that is, develops globally; Emerson concludes this paragraph with imagery that dramatizes his own self-birth. Here, Emerson becomes what he always already has been, his own father and son. This fact, more than any other about Emerson's personal coldness of temperament, explains the transcendental precondition that exists for him before all facts of experience: namely, that he, as a representative of the American subject, cannot have been affected passionately by his son's death or by any loss, since the self he possesses is not a property of any kind, but a quality, a motion, a self-renewing drive identical to the vision of the imaginative life itself:

> When I converse with a profound mind, or if at a time being alone have good thoughts, I do not at once arrive at satisfactions, as when being thirsty, I drink water, or go to the fire, being cold: no! but I am first apprized of my vicinity to a new and excellent origin of life. By persisting to read or to think, this region gives further sign of itself, as it were in flashes of light, in sudden discoveries of its profound beauty and repose, as if the clouds that covered it parted at intervals, and showed the approaching traveler the inland mountains, with the tranquil eternal meadows spread at their base, whereon flocks graze, and shepherds pipe and dance. But every insight from this realm of thought is felt as initial, and promises a sequel. I do not make it; I

arrive there, and behold what was there already. . . . I am ready to die out of nature, and be born again into this new yet unapproachable America I have found in the West. (169)

I hear innumerable echoes here—of Milton, Wordsworth, Shelley, Byron, and Blake—but I also detect the prefiguring of many to come, including among them Ashbery's previously cited formula, "the problem of pathos vs. experience."

Ashbery's "Self-Portrait in a Convex Mirror," whatever else it is doing, is also casting a cold eye on the quintessentially American project of self-creation: the recognition of the death of love as precondition for the birth of the self. Whatever Emerson's honesty in the matter may be said to be, out of shame alone, he and the American subject he would represent should just shut up, or at least be reduced to blank murmurings, like Ronald Reagan at the end. I think Ashbery would agree:

> The hand holds no chaulk
> And each part of the whole falls off
> And cannot know it knew, except
> Here and there, in cold pockets
> Of remembrance, whispers out of time. (83)

TIME OUT OF MIND

"Himself in Anachron," a sci-fi tale by Cordwainer Smith (a.k.a. Paul Linebarger),[8] perfectly sums up what I have read Auerbach, Cheever, and Ashbery as performing, what I call "the worldly apocalypse." There is an explicitly cosmic dimension to it, too.

Originally, this contribution to the *Lords and Ladies of the Instrumentality* cycle was to be published posthumously in *Galaxy*, the pulp magazine most supportive of Smith's work through the years. *Galaxy*'s circulation troubles in the mid-1970s, which prompted its submission, also caused its publication to be postponed repeatedly until the magazine went out of business. The story was in draft form and was prepared for publication by Smith's second wife, Genevieve, who finally put it in the omnibus collection of his tales, *The Rediscovery of Man* (1993). It subsequently was published in *When People Fell* (2007).

It is essential Smith and tells the story of Tasco Magnon and his new wife, Dita, who on their honeymoon have undertaken a mission for the Instrumentality into the mysterious Knot of Time. They are to gain there as much information as their instruments can garner about this curious Knot, but despite their best calculations, their time-traveling vehicle is bearing too much weight. After ejecting as much of the ship's contents as possible, even their food, they realize that one of them must make the leap into "anachron," the realm in between the Probabilities, from which no one has ever returned. This realm is the space beyond all imagination between one quantum probability of the breaking wave function and another in the sum-over history of infinite probability that collapses when one course is "chosen" to be realized, rather than some other, by the quantum foam of particles. From experiments in quantum mechanics, we still believe that this is what happens each time an observer in an experiment performs the experiment, but also, presumably, when one probable course of a particle appears rather than any other.

Tasco takes the flying leap in anachron and finds that he is "back-timing" (234). From a gray impalpability to a worldscape moving backward in time, Tasco snaps into the intensely paradoxical and painful experience of two times at one—that of his continuing progression of bodily aging in his time-traveling suit even as he recognizes the panel of his history on this planet that the temple erected to him displays before it shows him arriving old and becoming young again, going back to the point of his birth as a shining god-like being in the amazed eyes of the people on this world. This is the case even as he moves inexorably to his old age and death and approaches his arrival point. That is, he is moving back in time, which is the time of his virtual death, to the point where the process of his growing younger and his birth into a god-like being for these people ironically coincide with that moment of his death. The following passage presents both Smith's version of the American dream into self-birth into a god Emerson celebrates and the tragic vision of the human cost of that dream James tragically critiques. As such, it encapsulates the post-human imagination, which now is materially realizing itself every day, albeit in biogeneticsm not time travel and its self-overcoming in the persistent reading of the future of humanity, according to the humanist vision:

> He was still back timing. He had passed the time of his arrival and resurrection in this world. The resurrection was wisely prophesied by the beings who built the palace, painted the wings and halo around him. He would die soon, in the remote past of this civilization. Long afterwards, centuries before his own death, his alien remains would fade into the system of this time-space locus; and in fading, they would seem to glow and to assemble. They must have been untouchable and beyond manipulation. The people who had built the palace and their forefathers had watched dust turn to skeleton, skeleton heave upright, skeleton become mummy, mummy become corpse, corpse become old man, old man become young—himself as he had left the spaceship. He had landed in his own tomb, his own temple. He had yet to fulfill the things these people had seen him do, and had recorded in the panels of the temple. Across his fatigue he felt a thrill of weary remote pride: he knew that he was sure to fulfill the godhood which these people had so faithfully recoded. He knew he would become young and glorious only to disappear. He'd done it, a few minutes or millennia ago. The clash of time within his body tore at him with peculiar pain. . . . The building glowed as it seemed to come nearer. The ages thrust against him. He thought, "I am Tasco Magnon and have been a god. I will become one again." But his last conscious thought was nothing grandiose. A glimpse of moon-pale hair, a half-turned cheek. In the aching lost silence of his own mind, he called. *Dita! Dita!* (210)

If we answer such an imperative call, we become not sufferers of our impossible apotheosis but actors in the worldly apocalypse of our human tragedies.

Part Three

THE EXALTED STATES OF READING

7

"MONSTROUS LEVITY"

Between Realism and Vision in Henry James

"THE STORY of a Masterpiece" (1868) and "The Liar" (1888) recount the same basic plot. An artist is involved in a romantic triangle.[1] He paints a portrait betraying the true character of one of the other members of the triangle. The artist's far-from-disinterested, rather ironic intention—resentment inspiring the appearance of art for art's sake—is to paint a psychological masterpiece unveiling the other's deceptiveness. In revenge for wounded pride, he seeks to hold up the woman or her new partner or perhaps both to public scorn. The familiar Oedipal triangle's final member (fiancé or husband) then destroys the all-too-successful picture by stabbing through it many times. In both stories the scene of the portrait's ultimate destruction, unwittingly but inexorably caused by the artist himself, is described with a strangely intense pleasure, with what I would call, borrowing the phrase from "The Liar," "monstrous levity." This affect and pattern, the more they are analyzed, will reveal a Satanic paradigm. Here, then, are the two climactic scenes in question:

> He looked about him with an angry despair, and his eye fell on a long, keen poniard, given him by a friend who had brought it in the East and which lay as an ornament on his mantel-shelf. He seized

it and thrust it, with barbarous glee, straight into the lovely face of the image. He dragged it downward, and made a long fissure in the living canvas. Then, with half a dozen strokes, he wantonly hacked it across. The act afforded him an immense relief. (*CS1* 241)[2]

— • —

At one and the same moment Lyon perceived that the object [the Captain] had seized was a small Eastern dagger and that he had plunged it into the canvas. He seemed animated by a sudden fury, for with extreme vigour of hand he dragged the instrument down (Lyon knew it to have no very fine edge) making a long, abominable gash. Then he plucked it out and dashed it again several times into the face of the likeness, exactly as if he were stabbing a human victim: it had the oddest effect—that of a sort of figurative suicide. In a few seconds more the Colonel had tossed the dagger away—he looked at it as he did so, as if he expected it to reek with blood—and hurried out of the place, closing the door after him.

The strangest part of all was—as will doubtless appear—that Oliver Lyon made no movement to save his picture. But he did not feel as if he were losing it or cared not if he were, so much more did he feel that he was gaining certitude. His old friend *was* ashamed of her husband, and he had made her so, and he had scored a great success, even though the picture had been reduced to rags. The revelation excited him so—as indeed the whole scene did—that when he came down the steps after the Colonel had gone he trembled with his happy agitation; he was dizzy and had to sit down a moment. The portrait had a dozen jagged wounds—the Colonel literally had hacked it to death. Lyon left it where it was, never touched it, scarcely looked at it; he only walked up and down his studio, still excited, for an hour. (*CS2* 362–63)[3]

These two climactic scenes, despite their perverse resemblances, primarily demonstrate the major difference between these two artist-tales. That difference, of course, is largely a matter of technique. In the earlier story, the reader shares the narrator's omniscient, disembodied gaze. In the later story, the reader shares the limited, embodied point of view of the artist himself as he spies on the scene before him. A corollary consequence of this technical difference is that "The Story of a Masterpiece" represents directly, as a simple whole, the strange pleasure taken in the portrait's destruction by the tale's generally sympathetic, albeit jealous, hero and shared with the narrator and reader alike, while "The Liar" displaces such pleasure onto others, splitting it between the Colonel and the mediating figure of the artist, who is now an ambiguous, if not diabolic, hero. Whether the critical reader of "The Liar" and its authorial intelligence are to participate in the passions of these characters is a question left ironically in suspense. Clearly, however, in the later story, James is revising, literally redoing, the earlier one according to his greater understanding of and mastery over his imaginative powers.

My question concerns the nature of the strange pleasure in these two artist-tales. "The Story of a Masterpiece" represents this pleasure as both murderous and more than a little tinged with erotic satisfaction. In "The Liar" the artist names the act of destruction "a sort of figurative suicide," but he also exudes a voyeuristic pleasure of such great intensity that he becomes dizzy and excited for an hour. The simple whole of pleasure shared alike by the reader/narrator couple and the hero in the earlier story is thereby explicitly divided in two in the later story, becoming redefined in the process as two different pleasures, which are then distributed and embodied by the portrait destroyer and the artist, respectively.

The earlier story, however, provides a clue to the identity of the original pleasure in one of its narrator's awkward asides: "The artistic half of [the painter's] nature exerted a lusty dominion over the human half-fed upon its disappointments and grew fat upon its joys and tribulations. This, indeed, is simply saying that the young man was a true artist" (*CS1* 233–34). What James's *The Sacred Fount* (1901) much later projects as a demonic, vampire-like relationship between lovers is here represented at its source in the split subject of the true artist, that is, the modern transcendental genius. For James, the latter demonically consumes the former, like any fire its fuel. Contemporary psychoanalysis names such radical, excessive pleasure, with its interfusion of Eros and Thanatos, "jouissance":

> *Jouissance,* and the corresponding verb *jouir,* refer to an extreme pleasure.... [*J*]*ouissance* is an enjoyment that always has a deadly

reference, a paradoxical pleasure, reaching an almost intolerable level of excitation. . . . Lacan refers to the subject of *jouissance* as "the fathomless thing capable of covering the whole spectrum of pain and pleasure. . . ." There is an element of horror present in *jouissance* connected with the erotics of the death drive and offering terrible promises, going beyond the pleasure principle. *Jouissance* is fundamentally linked with excess. This excess refers to a pure expenditure which serves no purpose and is of a negative order, an excess of sexuality and death. (73)[4]

What a comparative analysis of these two artist-tales so far suggests, then, is the driven nature of aesthetic pleasure for James and the technical method, the ironic manipulation of point of view he develops to represent it effectively, so as both to maximize and to master it imaginatively.

To put the matter somewhat schematically, the Jamesian subject shows itself to be split between the empirical person and the artistic demon or transcendental genius. This familiar romantic conception of the artist is then the source, the ground, for the projected divisions and distinguishing qualities distributed among the Jamesian characters. All their relationships, however, are determined by the original paradigm of demonic, vampiric self-relation of "the true artist" announced in "The Story of a Masterpiece." I would suggest that the biographical basis for James's internalization of such a demonic paradigm of self-relation may derive from his perception of the relationship between his parents, in which the "genius" of his Swedenborgian father got fat by feeding off the practical care of his indulgent mother.[5]

However that may be, these two artist-tales taken together also disclose what can most destroy love and what needs to be condemned. Both tales name that quality of soul "levity." The genius of the artist is defined, ironically enough, as being especially intimate with and so best able to detect and expose such levity. Here is how it is revealing in "The Story of a Masterpiece":

It seemed to Lennox [her fiancé] that some strangely potent agency had won from his mistress the confession of her inmost soul, and had written it there upon the canvas in firm yet passionate lines. Marian's person was lightness—her charm was lightness; could it be that her soul was levity too? Was she a creature without faith and without conscience? What else was the meaning of that horrible blankness and deadness that quenched the light in her eyes and stole the smile from her lips? (*CS1* 232)

Similarly, in "The Liar," the artist-figure definitively judges his former lover and her husband, who destroys his own portrait, as guilty of "monstrous levity" (*CS2* 369) for their conveniently displacing the responsibility for the crime onto a "wretched woman" and helpless innocent, a now chronically tipsy, Cockney artist-model, Miss Geraldine. In the earlier tale, the artist's genius is best able to wrest the quality of levity from "the most superficial, most heartless of women" (*CS1* 226), and render it for all to see in the picture; in the later tale, such levity, now portrayed as "monstrous," is the quality of the invented story about Miss Geraldine that most revolts the artist there, just as it inspires Lennox in the early tale to a murderously penetrative rage against the betraying portrait.

Why "levity," and what is its relationship to Jamesian jouissance? According to the *Oxford English Dictionary* online, levity is "the treatment of a serious matter with humour or lack of respect.— ORIGIN Latin *levitas*, from *levis* 'light.'"[6] Of course, such "light" refers to being the opposite of heavy, or *gravitas*, but I like to trope on it as a monstrous light but in a comic, lack-of-respect sort of vein. As such, it suggests to me the extremes of parody and travesty that are virtually of a demonic nature. A once Lucifer-like "light"(-ness) is now seriously grave and demonic, Satanic—or only apparently so. Another helpful clue to the identity of this levity can be found in "The Story of a Masterpiece." When the artist and his former fiancée are finally alone together as she sits for her portrait, this is how the young James renders the scene:

"Well, Miss Everett," said the painter, in accents which might have been tremulous if he had not exerted a strong effort to make them firm.

"Well, Mr. Baxter," said the young girl.

> And the two exchanged a long, firm glance, which at last ended in a smile—a smile which belonged decidedly to the family of the famous laugh of the two angels behind the altar in the temple. (*CS1* 220)

I have searched for what "the famous laugh of the two angels behind the altar at the temple" refers to but to no avail. It appears to express a secret erotic complicity, as if the two angels were Blakean or, better still, Swedenborgian.

Here is where the later story may cap speculation. "The Liar" presents Miss Geraldine—the name alludes to an implicit source in Samuel Taylor Coleridge's "Christabel," much as Robert Browning's "My Last Duchess" is explicitly discussed in the earlier tale—as an uncanny intruding figure. She steals in from the garden entry to Oliver Lyon's studio while he is painting Colonel Capadose, the husband of his former lover, Everina Brant, and asks for a job as an artist-model. Lyon recognizes her type, whose "blighted career or Interrupted profession" (*CS2* 355) has been destroyed by her alcoholism, as if he "had made her" (367), but he fails to recognize her as an individual, when she pointedly and poignantly notes "with rather a wounded manner, 'Well, you know you *'ave* 'ad me!'" Lyon responds coldly to this potential double entendre, "I don't remember you" (355). Geraldine continues as if she knows he knows her but reminds him of her name and address, just in case he wants to send her a postcard if he ever needs her again. This chance incident later in the story gives Everina and her husband the plausible basis in literal fact for their libelous fiction. But since Lyon has seen what has really happened because he was spying on them from behind some curtains on the rickety stair landing above the studio, the "monstrous levity" of their irresponsible invention is all for naught. Ironically, the literal omniscience present in the earlier tale has been given to the fictional artist in the later, limited third-person tale. But, of course, ultimately, James retains in principle total mastery of point of view in both cases. Monstrous levity, with a vengeance?

In any event, I think the scene of repressive non-recognition of Miss Geraldine in "The Liar" bears further probing. First of all, "the radical defect," the "*brutal*" provocative effect of the portrait in "The Story of a Masterpiece" on the jealous fiancé John Lennox resides, he says, in its giving "Miss Everett the look of a professional model" (*CS1* 230). Like actresses, professional artist-models were thought to be a bit unsavory by polite Victorian society. More important, the pathos of Miss Geraldine's non-recognition in the later story, when combined with the diabolic nature of the literary resonance peppering the surface of both artist-tales, recalls for me the following notorious scene, so formative for the modern visionary subject.[7]

>Hast thou forgot me then, and do I seem
>Now in thine eye so foul, once deemd so fair
>In Heav'n, when at th' Assembly, and in sight
>Of all the Seraphim with thee combin'd
>In bold conspiracy against Heav'ns King,
>All on a sudden miserable pain
>Surpris'd thee, dim thing eyes, and dizzie swum
>In darkenss, while thy head flames thick and fast
>Threw forth, till on the left side op'ning wide,
>Likest to thee in shape and count'nance bright,
>Then shining heav'nly fair, a Goddess arm'd
>Out of thy head I sprung; amazement seis'd
>All th' Host of Heav'n; back they recoild afraid
>At first, and call'd me *Sin,* and for a Sign
>Portentous held me; but a familiar grown,
>I pleas'd, and with attractive graces won
>The most averse, thee chiefly, who full oft
>Thy self in me thy perfect image viewing
>Becam'st enamour'd, and such joy thou took'st
>With me in secret, that my womb conceiv'd
>A growing burden
>
>>Pensive here I sat
>Alone, but long I sat not, till my womb
>Pregnant by thee, and now excessive grown
>Prodigious motion felt and rueful throes.
>At last this odious offspring whom thou seest
>Thing own begotten, breaking violent way
>Tore through my entrails, that with fear and pain

> Distorted, all my nether shape thus grew
> Transform'd: but he my inbred enemie
> Forth issued, brandishing his fatal Dart
> Made to destroy: I fled, and cry'd out *Death*;
> Hell trembl'd at the hideous Name, and sigh'd
> From all her Caves, and back resounded *Death*.
> (Milton 2.747–89)[8]

The "monstrous levity" that inspires the destructive and self-destructive jouissance of the split Jamesian subject is truly diabolic, demonic, entailing a lusty dominion. Or so, following the lead of these artist-tales, I would contend.

In doing so, however, I do not intend to imply that James's perfected art of realistic imitation, as in these scenes from "The Liar," can be subsumed by some Miltonic demonic archetype of visionary self-creation, the way Everina Brant, now Mrs. Clement Capadose, claims at the end of the story that no artistic portrait, even a masterpiece, can ever measure up to the great "original" of her husband, which she alone possesses (CS2 371). Nor would I suggest that the critic can simply read the Jamesian text allegorically, according to the key provided by Milton or any other visionary or theoretical source. Rather, I propose that, on the basis of these two artist-tales, we may begin to see how the Jamesian text seductively dangles, between realism and vision, in a truly demonic form of "monstrous levity." The exquisitely done euphuistic equivocation and double entendre, the deftly unresolved and irresolvable ambiguity hanging radically suspended in the country of blue: this is the figural gesture of irony that exercises lusty dominion over the art of the Jamesian text and defines the Jamesian subject. To identify the significance of James's text entirely with either its represented society or its imaginative auteur is not to rise to its challenge, since the non-identification with any one position is key to the sublime effectiveness of James's aesthetic imagination; as such neither the "old" Henry James of American literature studies nor the "other" Henry James of new Americanist critiques alone can grant us a firm grasp on this slippery figure.[9]

As a final rationale for this critical approach to James, I will turn to Alain Badiou's set theory, in which any set is founded upon the void; that is, the void is all that the set cannot contain and remain the set it is. The void can become manifest within the set only when the state of the situation is put into radical suspense, when the policing function of business-as-usual, the endless counting and putting into place of the set's elements, suffers a crisis, an emergency, and all the set's elements then hang in a delicate balance within the enlightening space of the set's void. Within this visionary scene, a new truth can emerge. James's ironic art discovers and opens up this very luminous void in the house of modern fiction to a monstrous levity indeed.

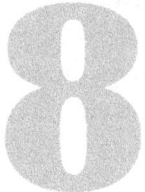

TOWARD A GLOBAL DEMOCRACY

James Baldwin and the Stoic Vision of Amor Fati

ONE OF Michel Foucault's final lecture courses, published recently as *The Hermeneutics of the Subject,* makes it clear that neither the historical Stoicism—that is, Stoicism in its time—nor the Stoic vision Foucault derives from it in this book is a retreat from politics into a purely self-regarding aesthetics of existence.[1] I will show that the Stoic vision Foucault wrestles from Hellenistic culture is one that has substantial promise for the emergence of global democracy. In order to make such a demonstration, some preliminary theoretical discussion is first necessary.

A classic scene concerning the nature of the self, from the history of the modern novel in English, is found in Henry James's *The Portrait of a Lady.*[2] Isabel Archer, the novel's young, newly rich American heroine, tells Madame Merle, an older, expatriate American divorcée and accomplished woman of the world, about the offers of marriage she has already entertained and rejected in her young womanhood. When Madame Merle asks about a recent suitor, inquiring about what his house looks like, Isabel is surprised and balks at the acquisitive intention inherent in such a question. Madame Merle, who is the female villain of the story, then explains what the Jamesian narrator terms her "metaphysics" (155). Every person comes equipped with her or her "shell" (156). In the case of Isabel's recent suitor, his "shell" is his house, which comprises "the envelope of circumstances that surrounds one" (156) and includes all the material manifestations of one's life. The self in Madame Merle's scheme of things exists in its material signs and can be read only from them. This self is not a whole greater than the sum of its parts; it is its parts loosely or strictly coordinated in response to social stimuli. All else is pure idealistic and speculative nonsense. Madame Merle is like a pragmatist semiotician, somewhat *avant le letter*.

Isabel objects to this view and claims instead that while she does not know if any of her things "express" her, even partially, she does know for sure they cannot exhaust who she is. Her things certainly do not act, for her, as a "measure" or standard that she tries to live up to, because she knows that social conventions, such as wearing clothes, can never truly express her self, since these are imposed on her by cultural norms and are not her free choice. The self, for Isabel, is greater than the sum of its parts. Moreover, her self is deeply interior and is only partially manifested in those few important choices that approach the conditions of being free ones. Isabel is a hermeneutic interpreter of consciousness and would be happy with her Puritan ancestors, Romantic cousins, or the Geneva School of Literary Criticism.

I invoke this scene from James because it allows me to make two fundamental points. The first is that however much one may want to believe Isabel is right about the self, she is not. Madame Merle is right. And the novel proves it, as Isabel continues to try to live as if she can entertain multiple possibilities forever, even as she recognizes later in her celebrated meditation (chapter 42) that her life has been reduced from the prospect of an infinite vista to dully staring at a dead wall (376). We too are constrained by the melodramatic plot of the novel to admit Isabel's reduction. By first running off to England, against her husband's wishes, to attend to her dying cousin, Ralph Touchett, and then bolting from the too-crude embrace of self-made manufacturer Caspar Goodwood back to Rome and her husband and her stepdaughter, Pansy, Isabel is like the prey in its lair, with one exit after another blocked by the uncanny hound. The second point on which Madame Merle is right and Isabel wrong is that the world of her time, her culture, and even more so that of our global culture of modernity function according to the logic of pragmatic semiology. That is, the deep self, existing outside of culture, has been shown to be most likely illusory, a mirage of language; but what is worse is that the contemporary world works whether or not the deep self does exist. In other words, it does not matter even if one could prove the hermeneutics of consciousness correct, as Isabel presents it. No one would use such proof in everyday calculations of opportunities to advance their interests. Madame Merle wins the argument every time today, as she does when Isabel says she does not choose to wear clothes but society requires it. And Madame Merle agrees, saying whether or not it is a free choice, no one goes about without them. How you act matters big time; what you say you intend matters little, if at all.

I realize that in this context it may appear ironic for me to be offering to your appreciation a book, *The Hermeneutics of the Subject,* if I do not believe in the usefulness, perhaps even the actual existence, of what such a book apparently presupposes, namely, Isabel's metaphysics and method of reading. But Foucault entitles the book as he does, and does not call it "the hermeneutics of the self," precisely to avoid such inadvertent irony. That is, he takes hermeneutics as being what the thinkers and writers he discusses are doing, or think they are doing, but not what he is doing. And he indicates this by using the word *subject* in his title and throughout the book, which is not a word his chosen thinkers and writers would have used. By *subject,* I take him to mean what the discourses he examines from the first centuries after Christ perform in their signifying structures and styles of thinking. If you imagine Madame Merle reading Marcus Aurelius, you have a rough idea of what Foucault is doing in this book.

In a central passage in *The Hermeneutics of the Subject,* Foucault clarifies this difference between self and subject, with respect to the most important topic in the book, what he calls *"le savoir de spiritualité."*

> As I have reminded you, within this general theme of conversion to the self and within this general prescription, "one must return to the self," I wanted to define the meaning given to the particular precept "turn your gaze on yourself," "turn your attention on yourself,"

"apply your mind to yourself." In posing this question and seeing how Seneca and Marcus Aurelius resolve it, it seems perfectly clear to me that it is not in any way a matter of constituting knowledge of the human being, of the soul, or of interiority, alongside, in opposition to, or against knowledge of the world. What, then, is involved is the modalization of the knowledge of things, with the following characteristics. First, it involves the subject changing his position, either rising to the summit of the universe to see it in itself totally, or striving to descend into the heart of things. In any case, the subject cannot properly know by remaining where he is. This is the second point, the first characteristic of this spiritual knowledge. Second, on the basis of this shift in the subject's position there is the possibility of grasping both the reality and the value of things. And what is meant by "value" is the place, relations and specific dimensions of things within the world, as well as their relation to, their importance for, and their real power over the human subject insofar as he is free. Third, this spiritual knowledge involves the subject's ability to see himself and grasp himself in his reality. It involves a kind of "self-viewing" ("*heauto-scopie*"). The subject must see himself in the truth of his being. Fourth, and finally, the effect of this knowledge on the subject is assured by the fact that the subject not only finds his freedom in it, but in his freedom he also finds a mode of being, which is one of happiness and of every perfection of which he is capable. In sum, knowledge involving these four conditions (the subject's change of position, the evaluation of things on the basis of their reality within the *kosmos,* the possibility of the subject seeing himself, and finally the subject's transfiguration through the effect of knowledge) constitutes, I believe, what could be called spiritual knowledge.[3]

Foucault goes on to say how it would be interesting to write the history of this spiritual knowledge (*le savoir de spiritualité*): how it was limited and then buried in successive waves, culminating in the sixteenth and seventeenth centuries, with Descartes, Pascal, and Spinoza, by the final full emergence of what he calls *le savoir de connaissance,* the knowledge of knowledge, or, as it is translated here, "intellectual knowledge,"[4] that is, knowledge of the conditions of any sort of knowledge, rather than knowledge with specific spiritual content or directives.

These four characteristics of spiritual knowledge that Foucault distinguishes form an interlinked action. From the subject's change of position to his evaluation of things based on their positions within the world, to the subject's seeing himself in this world, to the subject's transfiguration by such cumulative knowledge is what "return to self" means. Rather than some purely fanciful act of self-stylization, as if the subject were remodeling himself via the mirror of his concave interior, the subject recognizes his world and his position in it by means of substantially changing positions and viewpoints, literally and imaginatively, and that knowledge acts upon the subject to transform him from merely a passive observer into an active, participatory reader committed to the pursuit and experience of spiritual knowledge as it appears and affects the world. Think of a Madame Merle, with the heart of an Isabel. Only such a figure would be an appropriate mother for the innocent and fragile Pansy.

The Stoic vision of the cosmos, as seen from a new perspective by the subject, from either the heights or the depths, is intended to dislocate the subject from his familiar surroundings and habitual responses to radically new conditions that inspire or, better, provoke the subject into responding with new thinking, perhaps even creative thinking. This spiritual exercise is accompanied by more than mental traveling. The subject does not remain a provincial but becomes a cosmopolitan, not of the empire alone but of the world, indeed of the cosmos. The Stoic vision could be better named, perhaps, a cosmic or even a cosmological vision. In its self-imposed nature, this vision entails the kind of passionate attention to detail and the shape of the whole that the work of art does in its creation. The aesthetics of existence that Foucault celebrates in the final published volumes of *The History of Sexuality,* in which one is to view the self as a work of art, follows from the idea of the Stoic vision as outlined in *The Hermeneutics of the Subject.*

The subject's state of mind in this vision is what I would call, after Yeats's "A Prayer for My Daughter," "excited reverie."[5] It is a condition in which the subject experiences, to borrow psychoanalytic terms, both primary processes of the unconscious and secondary processes of the rational ego, simultaneously, the way the analyst and, presumably, the analysand do by the end of analysis. This mode of subjective self-consciousness is in fact as near to an objective experience of oneself that any person can have, and in certain circumstances, such as that of love, it may be made more readily available for more people than analysis, if only for brief and irregularly appearing moments at a time.

Consider, for example, the scene in James Baldwin's *Blues for Mister Charlie,* written in 1964 but not performed on Broadway until 1968, when, in act 1 Juanita confesses to Pete, another black student professor, that when Richard, the murdered blues musician whom she knew in childhood, had returned home, "he—hit—me in someplace I'd never been touched before."[6] She then explains:

> I don't mean—just physically. He took all my attention—the deepest attention. Maybe, that one person can give another. He needed me and he made a difference for me in this terrible world—do you see what I mean? And—it's funny—when I was with him, I didn't think of the future, I didn't dare. I didn't know if I could be strong enough to give him what he needed for as long as he would need it. It only lasted four or five days, Pete—four or five days, like a storm, like lightning! And what I saw during that storm I'll always see. Before that—I thought I knew what I was. But now I know that there are more things in me than I'll ever understand—.[7]

Whether we associate the sublime imagery of the storm with a transport to the heights or the depths of existence, we understand from the passage the scene of love's instruction in passionate attention. Such attention Yeats calls "excited reverie," and in one formulation or other, he identifies this "liminal" or "threshold" experience with vision.[8]

This transport is at once dreamlike and precisely focused, ecstatic and deeply immersed. In "Nineteen Nineteen," Yeats refers to this state as the "daemonic rage," which makes it sound more aggressive and intense than "excited reverie," but I think such differences are of degree, not kind. The affect Yeats is indicating, like Baldwin in the above passage, is a particular variation on the sublime: it is the state of mind of the creative moment, that moment when, fleetingly, the mind's components work together, however great the splits in the subject, and yet without reliance on habit or convention or automatism of any sort.

Foucault spells out the complicated nature of such passionate attention when he contrasts the eros of Plato, especially in *The Symposium* and *The Phaedrus,* which would rise to the heights of the Ideas, with the Stoic vision of Seneca. Seneca's eros is familiar to us now in the form of the Nietzschean *"amor fati."*[9]

> You can see that the movement outlined [in Seneca's *Natural Questions*] is not that of an effort by which we attempt to see another reality by detaching ourselves from this world of which we ourselves are parts. In other words, rather than a spiritual movement borne upwards by the impulses of eros and memory, what is involved is a completely different kind of effort, that of the real knowledge of the world, of placing ourselves so high that from this point, and below us, we can see the world in its general order, the tiny space we occupy within it, and the short time span we remain here. What is involved is a view from above (*une vue plogeante*) looking down on the self, rather than looking up to something other than the world in which we live. It is the self's view of itself from above which encompasses the world of which we are a past and which thus ensures the subject's freedom within this world itself. . . . [This vision] involves saying [to the subject] that there is no choice [among elements of the world] and that all the wonders to be found in heaven, in the stars and meteors, in the beauty of the earth, in the plains, in the sea and the mountains, are all inextricably bound up with the thousands of plagues of the body and soul, with wars, robbers, death and suffering. He is shown the world now so he can, like Plato's souls in *The Republic,* choose his destiny. He is shown the world precisely so that he clearly understands that there is no choice, that nothing can be chosen without choosing all the rest, that there is only one possible world, and that we are bound to this world. The only thing and the only point of choice is this . . . whether or not you want to live.[10]

The Stoic vision as exhibited in Seneca's *Natural Questions* and analyzed by Foucault is one that gives the subject the choice between embracing existence as it is, with its terrible mixture of elements, or not living. It makes stark the decision each subject must make: either one chooses to live and so love the world, doing the best one can within the terms of reality, or, preferring the vision of another unreal world of the pure good, whether deeply interior or high above, one refuses to be reborn into existence. Like Blake's title character from *The Book of Thel*, the subject confronts in the Stoic vision the choice of this world or the death-in-life of some perfect transcendent but nonexistent realm.[11]

This Stoic vision can work for Western, particularly U.S., citizens as the formative prolegomena to the democratic subject in our global epoch. The hundreds of millions of economically displaced peoples of the planet already know the literal experience of radical dislocation and the necessity to choose to live in a polyvalent world that the Stoic vision fosters in the name of a secular or worldly *amor fati*. One could argue that it is precisely the culture of security at all costs of the West and especially of the United States that, in reaction to such economic and other dislocations being brought back home, have provoked, via their total "war against terrorism," the very suicidal terrorism that culture would secure out of existence if it only could. Be that as it may, the effectiveness of the Stoic vision for any future global democracy lies, first of all, in its promise for educating in the ways of the world Western and U.S. subjects.

Once again, Baldwin's *Blues for Mister Charlie* provides a salient example. His opening stage directions set up the theatrical framework for performance that can maximize the experience of dislocation and the necessity to embrace life as it is, which implies not quietism but precisely the initial phase of a radical activism:

> Multiple set, the skeleton of which, in the first two acts, is the Negro church, and, in the third act, the courthouse. The church and the courthouse are on opposite sides of a southern street; the audience should always be aware, during the first two acts, of the dome of the courthouse and the American flag. During the final act, the audience should always be aware of the church, and the cross. The church is divided by an aisle. The street door upstage faces the audience. The pulpit is down stage, at an angle, so that the minister is simultaneously addressing the congregation and the audience. In the third act, the pulpit is replaced by the witness stand. This aisle also functions as the division between WHITETOWN and BLACKTOWN. The action among the blacks takes place on one side of the stage, the action among the whites on the opposite side of the stage—which is to

be remembered during the third act, which takes place, of course, in a segregated courtroom. This means that Richard's poem, Lyle's store, Papa D's joint, JO's Kitchen, etc., are to exist principally by suggestion, for these shouldn't be allowed to obliterate the skeleton, or, more accurately, perhaps, the framework, suggested above. For the murder scene, the aisle functions as a gulf. The stage should be built out, so that the audience reacts to the enormity of this gulf, and so that Richard, when he falls, he falls out of sight of the audience, like a stone, into the pit. In the darkness we hear a shot. Lights up slowly on Lyle, staring down at the ground. He looks around him, ends slowly and picks up Richard's body as though it were a sack. He carries him upstage, drops him.[12]

From these stage directions, we can see that the action of *Blues for Mister Charlie* will clearly involve ironic simultaneity, Proustian or Faulknerian flashbacks and flash-forwards, a theatrical approach to cinematic montage with the lighting up of different parts of the multiple set to play out different scenes in rapid succession, and in general a modernist aesthetic presentation and performance of the radical themes of the play. The play foregrounds especially the politics of the Black Power movement of the time, as it demonstrates the limits of the nonviolent approach of Martin Luther King Jr. and pushes the audience to embrace a more revolutionary project for race relations in the United States. Baldwin creates in this play a 1960s variation on the Stoic vision, with his world of terror and beauty, love and murder, racial hatred and religious delusion. It is this latter-day cosmos that we, the audience, must choose to embrace and live in, so as to do what we can, or, if we choose to reject and flee from it, we will continue to live without the passionate attention of love and sink, as largely the United States has, into the undead life of willful ignorance in the deluded culture of security.

Lionel Trilling, in a once-famous essay on *The Princess Casamassima,* invokes the trope of "the Young Man from the Provinces," by which he means that "the defining hero" in "the very backbone" of nineteenth-century fiction may come from any class but begins his career with a narrower mind-set than that with which he ends it.[13] Regardless of gender or race, apparently, this figure, according to Trilling, "starts with a great demand upon life and great wonder about its complexity and promise. He may be of good family but he must be poor. He is intelligent, or at least aware, but not at all shrewd in worldly matters. He must have acquired a certain amount of education, should have learned something about life from books, although not the truth."[14] We can think of many such novels in the history of the genre, most saliently James Joyce's *A Portrait of the Artist as a Young Man* (although it is of the twentieth century). Such a protagonist, whether an artist or not, must go through the terrible discipline of culture by which the mind receives its education, which bears a striking resemblance to the Stoic vision of learned humility in the face of the greater forces of society and life, which leads not to despair or defeatism, however, but to a salutary realism, what Trilling identifies as moral realism.

Baldwin's life exemplifies the story of this figure of the Young Man from the Provinces, as his own accounts and those of his biographers make clear. But what they have not made clear is that Baldwin's work, whether fiction or drama, essay or review, generally depicts the failure of this figure to survive being black in mid-twentieth-century America. "Sonny's Blues," the story of a jazz musician apparently overcoming the odds and getting back to his music, is an important exception, but Sony's ultimate fate remains unclear and shadowed by threats. The fate of Rufus in *Another Country*, also a jazz musician, who jumps off the George Washington Bridge, something a friend of Baldwin's in fact did, is much more typical. Baldwin is telling us in his work something about this failure of traditional patterns of life to apply successfully to African Americans, and his telling us these things is part of his updated Stoic vision of an ordered if inhuman world not fitted to reward our demands or help us fulfill our promise. Unless we fully accept such a vision, one in which nature and capitalism cooperate to produce monsters, such as racism, we cannot hope to deal with ourselves and each other with the moral realism and humanity Trilling discusses and Baldwin performs. The democratic imperative can operate effectively and justly only given such vision.

Baldwin is not simply repaying the liberal white *Partisan Review* mentors of his earlier work with a slap in the face by portraying the failure of the Young Man from the Provinces figure to function successfully for African Americans. He is also, and more significantly, testifying to the need for his imaginative version of Black Power self-reliance. One of the standard views of Baldwin is that all his works replay his relationship with his stepfather, David Baldwin, whose first son and namesake died and whose later son by Baldwin's mother was also named David. What is not recognized is that in such a work as *The Amen Corner,* Baldwin does indeed replay this relationship, but in a way that avoids any dependency on the white world and transfigures the father-son relationship, making it a vehicle for black self-reliance based on his version of the Stoic vision.[15]

In act 2 of *The Amen Corner,* David and Luke Alexander, son and father, are talking about what led to Luke's return home, sick and defeated, on the verge of death, just as David has to choose between doing what his mother, Margaret, wants, following her lead and becoming a preacher in church, and doing what he wants, following Luke's lead into the world of jazz and blues. This scene of choice of vocation repeats itself in Baldwin again and again, and it is tied always to the capability of passionate attention inherent in the vision of *amor fati* found in the Stoic vision of self-education.

> *Luke:* Well, son, tell you one thing. Wasn't music put me here. The most terrible thing in a man's life, David, is when he's done lost everything that held him together—it's just gone and he can't find it. And it just as hollow as a basin when you strike it with your fist. Then that man start going down. If don't know hand reach out to help him, that man goes under. You know, David, it don't take much to hold a man together. A man can lose a whole lot, might look to everybody else he done lost so much that he ought to want to be dead, but he can keep on—he can even die with his head up, hell, as long as he got one thing. That one thing is *him,* David, who he is inside—and son, I don't believe no man ever got to that without somebody loved him. Somebody *looked* at him, looked *way* down in him and spied him way down there and showed him to himself—then started pulled, a-pulling of him up—so he could live. (Exhausted) Hold your head up, David. You'll have a life. Tell me there's all kinds of ways for ruined men to keep on living. You hears about guys sometimes who got a bullet in their guts and keep on running—running—spilling blood every inch, keeps running a long time—before they fall.

I don't know what keeps them going. Father—or something—something—something I never had. (A pause) So don't you think you got to end up like your daddy just because you want to join a band.

David: Daddy—weren't the music enough?

Luke: The music. Music is a moment. But life's a long time. In that moment, when it's good, when you really swinging—you joined to everything, to everybody, to skies and stars and every living thing. But music ain't kissing. Kissing's what you want to do. Music's what you got to do, *if* you got to do it. Question is how long you can keep up with the music when you ain't got nobody to kiss. You know, the music don't come out of the air, baby. It comes out of the man who's blowing it.

This is a rich exchange between father and son, and it highlights all that Baldwin did not have from his stepfather and all that his stepfather also needed. More than this, this scene performs the transmission of the Stoic vision of self-education in *amor fati*, the love of fate expressed in cosmic terms, in a sharply poignant way significantly inflected by the African American experience of the choice of vocation in mid-century America. The worldly interiorized self is literally turned inside out in this vision and made to see itself as part of a play of signs and relations among signs, given motor force by what Luke identifies specifically with acts of love. The passionate attention called forth by playing music must be accompanied by such vision empowered by "kissing"—as Luke puts it, "what you want to do"—as well as by music, one's art and vocation, something "you got to do."

Any would-be democratic subject emerging especially out of the U.S. context and acting upon the global stage must pass through this process whereby one can turn inside out the narcissistic illusions of person, family, kin, race, and nation, any supposed deep interiority becoming a tissue of signifying relationships that potentially stop nowhere, being cosmic in their scope. The self-mystifying innocence and narrow-minded idealism of the American subject may then be reduced to and exposed as the imperialistic mechanized nothingness that it is. Only then may U.S. subjects, and hopefully the rest of the world, be worthy of true global democracy.

9

BRINGING OUT THE TERROR

James Purdy and the Culture of Vision

TOWARD A POETICS OF TERROR

My aim in this chapter, beyond attempting to read well a recent story by James Purdy, is to contribute to the large-scale and long-term critical project of elaborating a poetics compatible with what I take to be representative visionary projects.[1]

The classic modern statement of the writer's passion for vision appears in W. B. Yeats's 1917 "mythology," *Per Amica Silentia Lunae:* "I shall find the dark grow luminous, the void fruitful when I understand that I have nothing, that the ringers in the tower have appointed for the hymen of the soul a passing bell."[2] The condition of being completely undone, at an absolute loss, perfectly destitute, without resources of tradition or status, caught in the grip of not knowing whither or what, and, in terror, expecting some sort of total violation—this is, for Yeats, the tragic precondition of visionary creation. As Yeats's gothic figures of speech suggest, being rather like the damsel in distress of chivalric romance defines the moment immediately prior to ineluctable ravishment by—for him—a supernatural demon or beast. Imagine, in a different setting, the instant the sudden blow of the Divine Swan struck Leda. This moment is the terror of vision, out of which transgressive experience gives birth to something monstrous, uncanny, but also strangely beautiful, "a terrible beauty," as Yeats famously calls it in "Easter 1916."

The big difference between Leda and Yeats is that the poet, unlike the girl, courts vision's terror, while she has it literally befall her out of the blue. In this text, Yeats tells how the aging writer ascends to some waste room in his tower in search of any scrap of writing, "else forgotten there by youth," as he puts it, "some bitter crust" (15), on which the present-day older writer may feed for imaginative sustenance while awaiting, one more time, the spark of heaven to fall. Rather gnaw upon such stale crusts than end one's days like William Wordsworth, sappily sentimental and empty-witted, writing hundreds of sonnets about the history of the Anglican Church. When ecstasy is the goal of the quest, the visionary imagination is prepared to sacrifice all else.

Like Yeats, Purdy pursues such a project of vision. The problem for the critic is how to talk about it, especially to the great public who are not schooled in Byzantium or its American equivalents (if any, now). My current work concerns how to represent effectively for general critical discussion the dimension of the visionary in such writers as Yeats and Purdy, without reductive popularization or unwitting obscurantism. In this connection, ironically enough, given his notorious reputation, Jacques Lacan's psychoanalytic theories of the human subject, especially those in his later *Seminar* volumes, have been selectively useful to me.

The later Lacan permits me to describe the terror of vision as the jouissance of the real, that is, as that painfully compelling yet perversely enjoyable experience of acute anxiety. For Lacan, this anxiety or anguish arises not from the absence of all specific objects but precisely from the uncontrollable and imminent presence of the object or event that you know must render you absolutely helpless. Rather than envisioning the simulacrum of such an object or event—the leap off the cliff with bungee cord unrolling and cameras going, as on *Fear Factor*—just imagine taking a flying leap into the blackness, without any defenses or safety devices. Such libidinally invested, potentially suicidal acts bring out the terror of both Leda and Zeus. Such experiences of what Lacan calls the real constitute, via these works that prophetically and perversely celebrate it, like those of Yeats or Purdy, the culture of vision. In this culture, the real possesses and overwhelms all would-be masters and slaves.

I stress this ecstatic dimension of literature not gratuitously; when I awake in the middle of the night now, I do so in terror that having fallen asleep I may have been transformed into one of those alien beings I rail against during the day. The succubi I fear are not the pod people but the "security sheep." Who are they? They are those Americans who, since 9/11, deny the present, revise the past, and hope to preclude any new future emerging, all in the name of a perfected total security so exceptionally averse to life and its risks that they would coerce a new, nonhuman species into existence before our very eyes. It is my hope that literature, especially tragic literature, such as that of Yeats, James, Purdy, or Nathaniel Hawthorne, can withstand this new culture of security and in the end help to overcome it, provided we know how to speak about it clearly and truthfully.

According to Slavoj Žižek, we can readily recognize the culture of vision, in which literature and the arts participate, in Alfred Hitchcock's films, for they disclose the uncanny presence of the Lacanian *sinthome,* a term I will explain following this quotation from the recently revised edition of Žižek's *Enjoy Your Symptom:*

> Hitchcock did not proceed from the plot to its translation into cinematic audio-visual terms. He rather started with a set of (usually visual) motifs that haunted his imagination, which imposed themselves as his sinthoms [*sic*]; he then constructed a narrative that served as the pretext for their use. These sinthoms [*sic*] provide the specific flair, the substantial density of the cinematic texture of Hitchcock films: without them we would have a lifeless formal narrative. [Hitchcock] invented stories in order to be able to shoot a certain scene.[3]

However paradoxically ironic it may appear, this technical term, *le sinthome* (for some reason Žižek cuts off the *e*), works effectively to clarify the jouissance of the real. For what Lacan, in his late work, means in particular by *le sinthome* is this: it is a material form, evacuated of any rationally communicable meaning by its overdetermined and fragmentary nature, in which we nonetheless invest libidinally, erotically, with a fierce joy, or jouissance, even to a terrifying point of self-shattering and self-subjecting ecstasy. *Le sinthome* materializes jouissance in the very medium of the art form. It is not simply a fancy name for a fetish. At the core of subjective existence are these psychophysical kernels of pure irrationality—both contingent and fated—gaps in the symbolic order of social life, recalcitrant remainders (and reminders) of our infantile personalities that punch holes in the tissue of imaginary fantasies we would impose upon others and upon ourselves. These *sinthomes* (née symptoms) of the failures of repression (and so the promised guarantees of the inevitable ironic return of the repressed) become the hooks on which much of what we do not want to deal with gets caught. Rather than attempt to assimilate such symptomatic phenomena into a larger logic, Lacan would have us learn to enjoy them in their aesthetic forms as the compositional elements out of which works of art arise, artworks that can stitch together in ever new patterns the configuration of our psyches. Lacan had originally defined his view of sublimation as a form of idealization, but in his late work he revises that definition and presents sublimation as the material practice of an art that would transform the artist into the expression of his or her revised medium. This is one reason why Lacan renames the symptom *le sinthome*, especially with reference to the major example he analyzes in his 1975 *Seminar* "Joyce, the Symptom." If *le sinthome* sutures, with openly and increasingly nonsensical material, as Lacan thinks *Finnegans Wake* does, the structures of the psyche, then, without this supplemental operation, would fall apart, nothing more than the crimson wave thudding at sunset on the beach. Although like motifs in the way they carry through the story of a life, *sinthomes* are different in this respect, especially: they are not keyed to any communally recognizable codebook of symbolic meanings, and they tend to explode or subvert in other ways the imaginary fantasies we practice on ourselves and others.

Žižek reminds us that Hitchcock stages one particular *sinthome* repeatedly. A hand is offered to another, to save the other, but that hand withdraws or slips the grasp, sometimes purposefully, sometimes by accident, as the figure of the other falls into an abyss. *Vertigo* (1958) offers the most memorable instance in Hitchcock's cinematic corpus, but there are both earlier and later variations in *Saboteur* (1941) and *North by Northwest* (1959).

Žižek concludes his abbreviated anatomy of *le sinthome* in Hitchcock with a surprising and most instructive turn: he quotes Joseph Stalin's deathbed gesture (from his daughter Svetlana's memoir), in which

> [Stalin, at] what seems like the very last moment . . . opened his eyes and cast a glance over everyone in the room. It was a terrible glance, insane or perhaps angry and full of fear of death and the unfamiliar faces of the doctors bent over him. The glance swept over everyone in a second. Then something incomprehensible and terrible happened that to this day I can't forget and don't understand. He suddenly lifted his left hand as though he were pointing to something up above and bringing down a curse on us all. The gesture was incomprehensible and full of menace, and no one could say to whom or what it might be directed. The next moment, after a final effort, the spirit wrenched itself free of the flesh.[4]

Žižek asks, "What, then, did this gesture mean?" He explains that "the Hitchcockian answer is *nothing*—yet this nothing was not an empty nothing, but the fullness of libidinal investment, a tic that gave body to a cipher of enjoyment."[5]

Scenes of such visionary tics, such incomprehensible gestures, such figurative traces of our so-called perverse enjoyment in formally producing these very gestures and scenes, are ultimately what the analytic focus on *le sinthome* allows us to see. Purdy's work has both performed these sorts of gestures over the years and so confronted the emerging culture of security with its own often unacknowledged and "symptomatic" truths. This is the major reason for that work's unconscionable neglect.

A formal anatomy of these signatures of the real in Purdy would highlight three significant types: (1) the repeated (and at points overwhelming) presence of all sorts of bodily fluids (and other liquids), but especially water spraying onto people; (2) the problematic of names and naming; and (3) somnambulism (sleepwalking) or other hypnotic states. (The very word *terror* and its variants perhaps could make up a fourth *sinthome*.) One of his initial stories, "Don't Call

Me by My Right Name" (1956), features all three major types of signatures of what I would define as impersonally driven subjective identity.[6]

In this very early story, Lois McBane, married to Frank Klein for six months, cannot abide her new name—Lois Klein—and refuses to use it. At a party, the two of them drunkenly fight about it, with Frank dreamily knocking her down as she repeatedly gets up again and again, always refusing to accept his name as hers. Blood and whiskey spill everywhere, as do tears. Lois receives, finally, a concussion for her resistance and can no longer get up on her own. But these efforts of opposition are not in support of some protofeminist ideal of woman's autonomy, nor is there any evidence of any bias on her part. Rather, for Lois, it is a purely formal matter of the *sound* of the name: she hates it.

Similarly, liquids (particularly bodily fluids), the problematic of naming, and a compelling dreamlike logic, as of a half-roused mind, haunt "Some of These Days," the lead-off story in the 1991 collection *The Candles of Your Eyes*.[7] The protagonist is a nameless twenty-year-old for most of the tale. On getting out of prison, where he was brain-damaged from a fight and thus has trouble remembering names, he seeks his older male patron, Sidney Fuller, a sometime musician and composer. Our hero has come to call Fuller his "landlord" and is seeking him out in order to make it up to him for all the pain and trouble that he, James Di Silva, has caused. Unable to find his "landlord" (or more often just "lord," for short), because he has forgotten Fuller's name, Di Silva virtually lives out his days in an all-night porn theater, a place similar to one that Fuller used to frequent. There, Di Silva permits the men to perform unprotected sex on him for months on end, for the little human contact it affords. Contracting HIV and "rescued" too late by social services personnel, Di Silva suddenly recalls his patron's name when he is asked his own, and then, ironically enough, gives his own name when asked to whom his belongings, his "legacy," should be sent when he dies.

More examples from this collection, or from across Purdy's career as a novelist, playwright, and poet, could be given of these three major types of formal signatures (spraying or exploding bodily—and other—fluids, the question of name and identity, and sleepwalking as the model of all autonomic response). In themselves, such *sinthomes* (or libidinally invested material figures) help to identify author and character, as Lacan in his 1975 *Seminar* on Joyce suggests. Purdy's story "Brawith," from the recent collection, *Moe's Villa and Other Stories*, is another case in point. What happens to its oddly named title character—a progressive case of literal liquidation—showcases the reduction of his body to being a sounding board or an echo chamber for the body's deep interior as it torturously turns itself inside out.

Before giving a reading of that tale, with its striking signatures of the real, as well as a sketch of its place in Purdy's work overall, I want to make a brief digression into my understanding of the present moment, politically and intellectually, which makes Purdy's work even more compelling and important to understand than ever before.

As the ad nauseam broadcasts of all the "ins and outs" of the Terri Schiavo case underscores, since 9/11, U.S. popular culture, not surprisingly, has been obsessed with terror, terrorism, destruction, and death in all its forms and ramifications. The exceptionally driven nature of this obsession is often paraded out under the banner of "a culture of life" (as if culture wasn't always also, necessarily, as Freud has shown, "a culture of death"), and it is tied to news cycles of varying lengths and the political manipulations of the usual rightist sort. Something, some ur-plot, some indivisible remainder of primal trauma, some void in the logics of representation and symbolic sacrifice (public and personal), must be at work here. Today, we appear to be painfully driven to learn how to love our self-destructive fates, personal and public alike, under the guise of an imperiously smarmy ethos of fundamentalist religiosity.

To put all this in some larger historical perspective I recall how Nietzsche predicted that the next few centuries after the nineteenth would be "the age of grand politics," a struggle among ideas attached to military machines to master the planet, a struggle that many think, for better or worse, the United States has now won—except for various so-called minor insurgencies, terrorist groups, and other outlaw types, of course. Whether truly actualized now or not, I am not alone or uniquely prescient in thinking that global domination by one national power is not a good idea for the future survival of our species (or any other, for that matter). One major reason is that given such domination, when that power goes down, it is likely to take the rest of the world with it. "The culture of vision" (or "the real"), then, is my term for that feeling of late modernity in which we all now exist: we all stand at the brink of such a potentially planetary down-going in which all material and ideological forces and structures are geared up for a final transformation of the human species into versions of Nietzsche's "Last Man," that security-crazed type of barely human being for whom all contingent risks, heroic passions, and tragic awareness are themselves perceived to be instruments of a cosmic terrorism that must be not only corrected, as Plato might suggest, but extirpated, wiped out, completely. The vicious anxiety of this now-chronic condition of "The Last Man" (and also "The Last Woman") modernity, long in the making, is the real global terror that informs the personal and political dimensions of contemporary lives, especially in the United States, what I would now call "Security/Terror Central," or, more simply, "the culture of security," with its ever-increasing numbers of "security sheep." Bringing out the real terror in this long-in-the-making personal and political condition of modernity, rather than affording us another ramshackle fictional or intellectual refuge from it, best describes, I think, the profound truth of Purdy's authentically visionary career, which is every bit as powerful and important, in my estimation, as that of Yeats, Hawthorne, or Blake.

THE IMPOSSIBLE SUBJECT: THE TRUTH OF THE REAL

Thanks to the James Purdy Society Web site, the Thomson Gale digital text *Contemporary Authors*, and Donald Pease and Warren French's entry on Purdy in Thomson Gale's *Dictionary of Literary Biography, Volume 2: American Novelists Since World War II*, critics have an archive of pertinent materials to begin with if they want to tackle Purdy's work. I will not rehearse again now the general outline of his career as a novelist, short story writer, dramatist, poet, and man of letters. Instead, I want to focus on a few of his statements in order to connect what I have said so far about his work and the present moment we inhabit with his most fundamental imaginative principles. To that end, I will begin with some statements Purdy makes in an interview conducted by Christopher Lane at Purdy's Brooklyn home on November 27, 1993.[8]

"I learned early on that the only subjects that I could possibly deal with were impossible.... Nearly all my books are based on 'impossible' subjects" (6). It is clear from the context that Purdy is referring not only to subjects in the sense of "topics" for literary treatment, but also to subjects as "characters" who pursue impossible courses of action. As such, Purdy, in Lane's helpful rephrasing a few lines further on, writes about subjects in their "enjoyment of the forbidden" and transgressive (8).

Unlike any popular notion of such things, however, as he goes on to elaborate, Purdy is after forbidden or transgressive *truths*. Speaking of one of the characters of his 1967 novel *Eustace Chisholm and the Works,* Purdy says that "his problem is everybody's problem. We can't face what is most ourselves, what is deepest in ourselves. Like Macduff, in *Macbeth,* who was from his mother's womb untimely ripped, we want to rip out the really delicate, beautiful things in us so that we will be acceptable to society.... It is [then] when we don't face ourselves that we become destructive" toward others and ourselves (10). Lane then adds, again most helpfully, "a lot of your characters are on boats that are sinking," and Purdy runs with this image, saying, "Almost all of them. I think humanity is always on a sinking ship. Certainly America is sinking with outrageous crimes that our government has perpetrated" (15). Unfortunately, this is even truer today. Purdy continues in this vein: "These [characters] are very desperate, confused people who are doing the best they can.... But I think if you look at anyone's life, their life is not correct—they're making one mistake after another. They're blundering, they're falling, they're hurting people" (16).

As Lane teases it forth from Purdy, "intimacy with someone is also about a non-relation with the person one apparently is involved with," or, as Purdy now revises Lane, "we may never know whom we're loving, and they don't know who is being loved" (16). Because of this fundamental nonrelation at the heart of all intimate relationships, Purdy's characters live lives in which truly, as Yeats would also have it but in Purdy's own words, "Eros is the violent god" (21). That is, as Lacan (following Freud's lead) sees it, jouissance melds death and life drives. As Lane puts the issue facing Purdy's characters, they "seem to be stuck between two options—either to pursue rapture and to try to live it out to the full [as possible delusional endurable joy] . . . or to confront its [inevitable] demise, and learn to do without, which is shattering and painful for them" (25).

Consider the beautiful moment in the midst of the stormy one-act play *Clearing the Forest* (1978), collected in *Proud Flesh* (1980). The two characters, Gil and Burk, confront each other, and Gil in particular confronts the truth about himself and their relationship, as they prepare dinner for the woman Gil plans to marry, because he thinks he cannot stand a life of "all storms and flashes of lightning."[9]

> *Gil (turns to the audience):* "I've heard of boys (*as if to himself*) who loved the storm even after they had been struck and singed by the lightning and drowned by the rain and deafened by the thunder . . . when the great summer thundershowers would be at their height whether in the dead of night, or before the dawn had come, they would steal out of their warm beds, and go into the clearing before the forest, and look up into the world eye of the tempest, they would hold their body and soul up to its destruction, not just once in a lifetime, but again, again, again!" (*He falls down on his knees and covers his face with his hands.*)

Burk's response to this vision is, simply, to come over to Gil, saying, "You deserted your lightning, your storm."[10]

Without going much further into this powerfully moving drama, I want to underscore the tragic alternatives presented in this scene. For as the play concludes, Gil stabs himself to death rather than embrace his "lightning," his "storm," or accept a conventional marriage of convenience, and so this tragic climax perfectly exemplifies Purdy's (and Lane's) points made in the interview cited about the choices open to "the impossible subject" in Purdy's work. My point here is this: the theme of the impossible subject is much akin to Lacan's conception of Antigone's drive not to cede ground with respect to her desire, and such a theme in both writer and theorist manifests itself first of all and essentially on the purely formal textual and structural levels as generic signatures of the real, here the semiautomatic vision of being struck dumb in the simplicity of the lightning's fire. It is just such *sinthomes* modern culture ironically disseminates and paradoxically disavows—only for them to return upon that culture, in fact upon the idea of culture itself, with a vengeance, sometimes, as now, with all the terror of apparently apocalyptic (self-)destructiveness.

In the present moment of human history, in the United States at least, the very possibility of facing such a tragic deadlock would be foreclosed. The goal of this total security mind-set (as far as I can see it) is to shape a populace for the future that could not even conceive of anything but such security and of any potential difference from it as terroristic impiety. If Purdy, like Yeats, envisions the creative writer as courting his tragic vision of evil and divine ravishment, at the risk of death itself, then Bushworld, ideally, would banish the seeds of all such visions precisely in the moment just prior to their being formed. Bushworld would perfect the prophylactics of the condom on a grand, indeed global, scale.

Rhetorically or compositionally speaking, Purdy's short story "Brawith" is most like a process essay. It lays out, step by painful step, with a few comically grotesque pratfalls along the way, the story of how its title character, perhaps named for a deserted medieval village in North Yorkshire, dissolves from the inside out due to his severely traumatic injuries from the war (which one does not matter). Brawith ends his days stuck up his grandmother's chimney and then wrapped in toilet tissue from head to toe, finally stepping out, bursting like a tsunami wave of blood, sweat, and tears (and other excretions), all of which cascade down all over her. The story's final coherent image of Brawith is that of a human tampon, his identity (like the absorbed contents) exploding out of the chimney in what is perhaps on one level a visionary allegory of toxic shock writ large. Because Purdy tells this strangely named story, which is certainly worthy of or even tops Blake, Poe, or Beckett at their surreally macabre best, with such precise and progressively appalling detail, in such relentlessly exacting and formally exquisite prose poetry, as if miming the pace of the dreaming sleepwalker, the reader is captivated and caught up in the anxious logic of the story right up to its terrible, long-postponed, and anxiety-ridden bitter end. The story within this story, that of the uncanny relationship between Brawith and his grandmother, Moira (which, of course, means "fate"), their unsymbolizable bond beyond all constraints of gender or generation, makes one think of some Greek tragedy or possibly an Old English folk tale of heroic suffering, taking place in that fabulous territory of legend, myth, and the White Goddess and her son (or grandson) that Robert Graves plumbed in his classic text on the subject of the sacrifice. Be that as it may, "Brawith" does clearly bring together those three signatures of the real, those *sinthomes* of fiercely enjoyed drive activity earlier noted: that of the overwhelming presence of precious bodily (and other) fluids; the problematic of the name, naming, and identity (Brawith is an orphan, having lost his parents some time ago); and the transformation of human agency into the inhuman agency of somnambulism—in this case, not only at the level of the narration itself, which proceeds as if according to the often nightmarish, slow-motion logic of sleepwalking. Since the story is told from the point of view of Moira, the reader is implicated in all the effects of Brawith's fate as they are unfolding upon her, literally in sheet after sheet of first sweat and then blood, urine, shit, and semen.

Moira rescues her grandson, Brawith, from the veterans hospital near where she lives in Flempton, Ohio. Her cousin Keith had persuaded her, against her better judgment at the time, to allow the Army to send Brawith there. Due to a bomb explosion of shrapnel and likely machine-gun fire, Brawith has internal injuries so severe that he is forced to carry a roll of toilet tissue around with him. To say he is incontinent is to practice understatement with a vengeance. Moira asks him one day while visiting him in the hospital if he wants to stay there or move into "grandmother's house" in the countryside near the copse, the river, and the woodlands. He reiterates the words "grandmother's house," nodding repeatedly.[11] Moira takes Brawith home with her. Once he is home with her, and she sees how his condition is progressively deteriorating—all he can do at first is mail her "government postcards" for her, and then not even that—Moira remains fixed in her initial decision. She expresses her doubts to herself, but rarely to Brawith. Before he dies, however, she does climactically ask him again if he wants to go back to the hospital, and he indicates he wants to stay with her.

Here is how the reader is introduced to what Moira comes to experience on a daily basis:

> Gradually it occurred even to her that he was slowly oozing from almost every pore in his body, and it was not that he did not think with words anymore, or not hear words, his attention was entirely occupied by the soft sounds like whispers arising from the wet parts of his insides, which shattered by wounds and hurts had begun gently coming out from within him or so it seemed, so that all his insides would one day peacefully come out; so his insides and his outer skin would merge finally into one complete wet mass. (177)

Naturally, this hope for a peaceful end is thwarted by the increasingly loud and painful reverse osmosis going on. But given just his initial condition of incontinence, why does Moira not return him to the hospital? One reason is typical human stubbornness, of not wanting to go back on a decision made against all sensible advice, so as to avoid having to have been told "I told you so" by her cousin and others. The other reason, however, is that Moira feels she and Brawith have established a bond, from which she receives great joy: "he was the only human being who looked up to her, and she would keep him by her side therefore. . . . Her reward came when he would once or twice a week, no more, look up at her and say '*Moira.*' It meant thank you, she supposed, it meant, even love, she felt" (177). Repeatedly, Moira now vows to herself that "nothing is too good for you, Brawith," that he is the only person she now or ever would do anything for, and that due to his sacrifice, the community should honor him, and that if the community won't do so, or can't somehow, she will do it (180).

One day, however, as she is cleaning his feet in a basin, the soft sounds of his insides leaking out grow much louder:

> She paused for a moment, incredulous, fearful, yet at the same time she could share his knowledge. She listened carefully and she heard enough [being somewhat deaf in one ear] of the many sounds that were coming from inside himself and which he listened to constantly. All this she was now aware of. Their eyes met briefly, and he gave her a kind of nod, meaning he knew she had heard the sounds and had understood. She held his feet in a tight clasp. That [moment] was the beginning of their even deeper closeness. (181)

Although in this situation, there is considerable leeway for misconstruing on her part, that last sentence appears to endorse Moira's view of things from the narrator's perspective. I take this to be significant, because not only are Moira and Brawith increasingly beyond the conventional symbolic order of society, despite being still dependent on its operations for their necessities (such as food deliveries), but Moira and Brawith are also, at this point and until his death, beyond the imaginary misreadings of projective identification and personal fantasy.

These two characters are living out their unsymbolizable bond in what Lacan calls "the real," that domain of pure drive activity that informs but also is analytically prior to even the primary processes of the unconscious:

> Nothing is too good for you my darling. She felt he heard her, though she was beginning to understand that at last all he heard, all he felt, all he knew was the communications which the vast flowing we of his insides imparted to him, those rivulets of blood and lymph, the outpouring of his arteries and veins, all of which whispered and told him of irreparable damage and despair, and of the awesome future that was to come. (180)

As they both are sleepless, they spend their nights together listening to these sounds, and as they get louder and louder, more authoritative and commanding, like the voice of conscience or of impulse, they establish communication between them by means of these sounds suddenly getting louder in response to her question or remark, and then subsiding again: a kind of natural language of abjection.

As she comes out of a brief doze one morning, Moira hears "some new sounds arising from the fireplace" (183). Now, Brawith can barely hear anything, she says, and she can hardly hear herself think, as "the sounds of his own swimming insides drowned out all other sound," reverberating as they do from the chimney to envelop the house inside and out. Once again, despite her own piercingly poignant misgivings, she refuses to go back on her decision and cede any ground to social norms or common sense, and realizes that, in a comically painful pun, "she had never loved anybody with such complete absorption as she did Brawith. She felt her own insides cried out along with his" (184). Are we to mention Moira and Brawith in the same breath with SpongeBob and Patrick? However that may be, this is the moment when she asks him one last time whether he wants to return to the hospital, but she interprets his sudden uncanny silence as meaning "he would not wish to return" (185). So she welcomes his unspoken word "more than sunshine" (185), as her feminine gaze "hears," rather than reads, what the sign of his absent gesture ironically signifies.

At this point in the story, however, Purdy introduces a strong caveat to the reader's taking Moira's view of things without question, when he has her reflect enthusiastically that she "felt now that he had come to her of his own free will, that she had not prevailed on him to join her here at the outskirts of Flempton, that he had in fact written her asking to join her in her home. She had never known such happiness, such calm, such useful tasks" (185). Of course, Brawith had never written her anything of the kind. While the other interpretations prior to that statement may be plausibly correct, that statement is dead wrong, and so it begins to make us recall other of her readings that may have skewed the truth so that she might feel useful and important to someone, such as the following, which can appropriately represent the others:

> "He has given his all," Moira was heard again and again to retort on the phone to Lily [her sister], and as she said these words Brawith looked over at her, and something almost like a smile passed over his blurred lips, for there was never any real expression on his face—all there was of expression must have been kept now in the depths of his insides which nudged and urged more and more to come out, to be released themselves like a sheet which would cover his outside skin and hair. (179)

And yet, as they are "sleepless together in the darkness," and as she hums and sings songs to him all night and day "rather than say anything to him in ordinary speech" (181), we have to wonder if Moira is really wrong in terms of the spirit of their relationship now. Similarly, as "his brow became more and more sopping wet the

CHAPTER 9 | BRINGING OUT THE TERROR

voices inside his body grew more insistent, more authoritative. She felt they were crying out for something withheld from him" (183). Is Moira wrong here? Apparently not, given the narrator's comment at the conclusion of the following passage: "At first spitting out his food before swallowing it, after eagerly gobbling up, Brawith ends unable to chew at all but just spits out anything put in his mouth," as Moira and he sit "listening to the dictatorial sounds issuing from inside him. Grandmother and grandson were pushed into deeper silence as if they sat before a political orator or a preacher of the gospel" (183). Both share in the abjection of authority.

Refusing to come out of the fireplace, with his head stuck up the chimney, Brawith is becoming too weak to stand all day and night, and so Moira, having already moved her cot to be with him, holds him up while he turns into a quivering mass, scratching and clawing at the brick of the chimney, but instead of dust coming down, now "Moira saw a sheet of sweat descending as if from a broken pipe, and this was followed by actual sheets of blood" (186). Despite all this, she "felt she must hold him up into the body of the chimney since this was his wish" (186).

As the climax (or better, "the end") is coming on, Moira asks Brawith if he wants her to do anything different from what she is doing, and showing that he does still communicate with her, he all at once lowers "his head from inside the chimney and pointed with a kind of queer majesty with one hand toward a roll of toilet paper" (187). As the reader knows, Brawith always carried one with him everywhere, even sitting in a rocker and holding a roll on his lap as he would rock the night away. (Just imagine the radically parodic effects of him approaching townsfolk, carrying his roll of toilet tissue in his hand.) Brawith wants it now so he may cover over his entire body, mummy-like. At first appearing naked to Moira, looking again, she realizes that his skin and clothes and insides are now all the same color and wetness, "as his skin [is] breaking totally now," exposing his insides (187). Nonetheless, Brawith manages to put over the worst of "the bursting places" sheets of toilet paper that now are turning red immediately "from the wet stuff that was now bursting from within his entire body" (188). Despite this savagely grim spectacle, Moira manages to wonder with a blackly humorous bemusement what would happen when "the last roll was consumed" (188).

The story concludes with the depiction of the act of death and its immediate aftermath like none other in the history of literature, and I will cite it in its entirety for its powerful effect, which will strongly inform and support my own conclusion. These last three paragraphs are all punctuated, like a good process-analysis essay, by the transitional term *then*.

> Then she thought she heard him scream, but she realized that the many noises and sounds which had been audible within his body were moving now up to his larynx and causing his vocal cords to vibrate as if he were speaking.
> Then she fancied he did speak one word or part of an unfinished phrase: "*Deliver!*" repeated again and again: "*Deliver.*"
> Then like a flock of birds the terrible noise seemed to rush over her head deafening her. She fell, losing hold on his legs, and as she did so an immense shower of blood and intestines covered her, and his body entirely wrapped in toilet paper from head to toe fell heavily on her. Moira did not know how she was able to rise and finally make her toilsome way to the side porch where Mr. Kwis was waiting with anxious dread. She hardly needed to tell him her grandson was no more. In silence Mr. Kwis took her hands in his and pressed them to his lips. Then speaking in a faint whisper, he said he would go now to tell those who were concerned that the heavy burden of Brawith's life had been lifted at last. (188)

So many possible interpretations of this story and its conclusion arise now that the mind is boggled, and yet the action is as simple as can be, both appalling and grotesquely comic at once. The reader can conjecture with every plausible rationale, especially given the Yeatsian visionary context I began with, that Brawith in the chimney is returning to the womb, or at least the birth canal, and Moira is acting as midwife to his rebirth into that other name for either living death or salvation: "*Deliver!*" Or, as a friend recently suggested to me, a reader may hear in the name *Kwis* an intimation of what the leaking of Brawith's insides into the outside world must have first sounded like.

The best way to sum up "Brawith" and this conclusion is to suggest that not only does Purdy here gather together three of his most formative signatures (or master figurative *sinthomes*), but he also presents, with his typical "in-your-face" flair, the real dimensions of the ultimate human experience. Beyond this, I think, he also dramatizes rather quietly, amid all the fundamental sounds, what it would mean to have existing between two people an unsymbolizable bond in the domain of what Lacan calls "the real" of primary drive activities. That is, beyond the conventional imperatives of certainly any modern culture, beyond the traversable, too-often-flimsy fantasies of individual desires, we have here in "Brawith" the pure form of an unspeakable and strangely impersonal intimacy. Such an uncanny intimacy, if broadly practiced, would confront and defeat our culture of security with that original "weapon" of mass creation: the truly visionary human imagination.

conclusion

THE TRUTH OF
AMERICAN MADNESS

On Love and Vision in The Golden Bowl

THERE IS A moment in *The Golden Bowl* (1904), Henry James's famously difficult, final novel, in which Prince Amerigo, despite the sharp differences he perceives between himself and all the Americans he is involved with, contemplates his situation with pleasure and amusement.[1] An Italian prince whose ancestors have squandered the family wealth, Amerigo has married Maggie, the only daughter of an American billionaire, Adam Verver, who has given up making money for spending it on art. Verver's "supreme idea" (109), as he calls it, is to place the best representations of human civilization in the museum he has built back in his hometown of American City, and, as we learn, Verver has a special eye for what counts as "the real thing" in business or in art. Amerigo's generous father-in-law has provided the substantial funds to bail out Amerigo's family from their debts, and then some, based on his judgment that Amerigo is precisely the authentic item.

Meanwhile, Maggie, with Amerigo's friend Fanny Assingham's help, has provided him with a most agreeable new mother-in-law, Charlotte Stant, Amerigo's former lover, who is also Maggie's best friend. Now that Maggie presumably will not be there to protect him, Adam will not have to deal with importunate gold-digging women who are auditioning to replace his long-dead first wife, once the father and the daughter decide to bring Charlotte in to clean house, as it were.

Amidst such psychologically incestuous complications, Amerigo pauses to reflect, not so much on his uncanny good fortune as on how, despite his several years dealing with all these Americans, he does not really understand them at all:

> Those people—and his free synthesis lumped together capitalists and bankers, retired men of business, illustrious collectors, American fathers-in-law, American fathers, little American daughters, little American wives—those people were all the same large lucky group, as one might say, they were all at least of the same general species and had the same general instincts; they hung together, they passed each other the word, they spoke each other's language, they did each other "turns." (218)

Amerigo's casual observation is in fact an important one, as I will argue.

The difference between Americans and Amerigo is that between two species—a mutation in human nature, at least, in the form of life. And if we take that phrase seriously, then a people living in the same place and practicing the same increasingly new form of life can transform the human subject in ways that can make it appear like a new and different species. Wherein lies this salient figurative difference, which is now, thanks to imperialism and globalization, spreading around the world and is increasingly making all human beings not so different, as other forms of human life are killed off, or "radically transformed," as the popular pundits say?

The primary mark of difference between Amerigo and the Americans (ironically enough given his distant familial ties to the ancient explorer for whom their continent is named) lies in the form of subjectivity. Amerigo, early in the novel, explains to his fiancée that there are "two parts of me" (9); the larger part is the family history, not its genetic structure but the genealogical record of what his ancestors have done in history. Their actions and those consequences have been inscribed into his individual subject. So powerful is this historical second nature that at times in the novel the ghost of one ancestor or another takes over Amerigo's facial appearance, gazing out spectrally upon the world once again. There is "another part, very much smaller doubtless," Amerigo then admits, "which, such as it is, represents my single self, the unknown, unimportant—unimportant save to *you*—personal quantity" (9).

It is this unknown individual part, given by nature and strengthened in the notorious absence of long-standing authoritative institutions, of which the Americans are primarily made. Amerigo views this unknown part of himself with suspicion for its possible irrationalities, which are the result of its inability to be adjusted to the historical realities of human life in society. The Americans, on the other hand, possess to their self-conscious knowledge largely nothing else but this unknown representation or private imagination of their single self, and they assume it is largely good, and naturally moral: "like a dazzling curtain of light" (19), it is "the colour of milk or snow" (19). It is as if what Americans do in the world and all the consequences of such action cannot touch or penetrate this "great white curtain" (19), dividing their true selves from the world in which the rest of human beings live. Amerigo's father-in-law, for instance, modeled on Andrew Carnegie in many respects, aches for the vision of this "impersonal whiteness" of pure innocence when he falls prey to potential social complications. He is said to riffle the Golden Isles, with his daughter, of all of Europe's art, much as, in Gilded Age robber-baron fashion, he made his many billions via capitalist exploitation. Such a literally transcendental self-imagination by Americans—transcendent of all ensnaring circumstances—Amerigo can perceive, even as he cannot begin to understand it.

We are given a more precise formulation of the difference between Amerigo's historically representative tragic mode of human subjectivity from the new romantic American subject, when the Jamesian narrator, taking his cue from his character Adam Verver's supreme idea of connoisseurship, nominates "the aesthetic principle" as what marks this difference (147–48). A new measure of all value is what this aesthetic principle is, and it defines Adam Verver's life in both its productive and consumptive phases as capitalist and connoisseur, respectively. It is as if, the text says, Adam Verver had the same glass lens—presumably like a jeweler's loupe for judging the quality of gemstones—to use for determining the reality or authenticity of a financial opportunity or a fancy statute (147), and yet the object in question is said to fill the glass like a fluid in a fancy sipping utensil.

On the face of it, however, this mark of difference, the aesthetic principle being applied to all of life as the universal measure of all value, does not really fly. The idea of the aesthetic principle as a substitute for the religious principle as the end-all and be-all of value judgments comes originally, after all, from Europe, whether we trace it back to the romantics there or to the generation of the symbolists and aesthetes and decadents. Certainly, Amerigo is no stranger to its workings of the aesthetic principle, or to recognizing his father-in-law's successes. I think the difference, which the introduction of the aesthetic principle both discovers (because it does tend to flatten out history's three-dimensional solidities into a series of images) and obscures (because this operation distracts from what is really happening on a deeper level of human subjectivity), is that of the split subject and how the American responds to that fact of civilized life.

We know from anthropologists and psychoanalysts that civilization in the shape of human culture requires that each subject be formed out of a split between the person and the performance. This split occurs between the individual and the role, or the unknown part and the portion determined by the symbolic linguistic and discursive networks of family, religion, class or social group, people, nation, culture, and so on. On the evidence of *The Golden Bowl,* Americans both deny the existence of such a split and fill it in when it appears so that as an aesthetic appearance the subject is innocent of all fracture or penetration. As Maggie Verver puts her highest (albeit remedial) desire, late in the novel: "The golden bowl—as it *was* to have been" (462). So, the aesthetic principle as the highest and only principle of valuation does lead us to recognize the American difference, but whereas the good European accepts the necessarily unfulfilling nature of life, the good American disavows that vision as impossible. Furthermore, the American would use all available material resources to make the ideal vision of innocent perfection, paradise on earth. The human subject must be perfect to begin with and perfected always—both, insanely, at once. We can call this national insanity of our would-be super- (or post-)human state, however it may also appear elsewhere and else-when (as in the Roman proclivity to deify the emperors they just killed), the exceptionally American madness. As we have seen in previous chapters, the cost of this American vision of a quintessentially undivided state of being is the loss of love as we have known it in human history, a loss that makes possible, perhaps, the planetary acquisition and hegemony of late capitalism and its new form of life.

James stages the recognition of the American madness as a vision of perfection at the price of love, and he does so, ironically, as Maggie testifies to her father about her discovery of the three modes of love and how they are intimately tied to three forms of jealousy. She has made this multifold discovery through her painful confrontation of her husband's and her mother-in-law's adultery. Maggie purchases and subsequently speaks with the shopkeeper who sold her the same golden bowl Amerigo and Charlotte memorably passed on as a gift for her wedding four years previously because of the crack in its gilded crystal. As Maggie and Adam are meeting to arrange the future for themselves and of their wayward spouses, without speaking directly about what would ruin the precarious equilibrium of their collective life, Maggie remarks on these three kinds of love and jealousy:

> My idea is this, that when you only love a little you're naturally not jealous—or are only jealous a little, so that it doesn't matter. But when you love in a deeper and intenser way, then you're in the very same proportion jealous; your jealousy has intensity and, no doubt, ferocity. When however you love in the most abysmal and unutterable way of all—why then you're beyond everything, and nothing can pull you down. (495)

After a significant pause, her father responds:

> "I guess I've never been jealous," and it said more to her, he had occasion next to perceive, than he was intending: for it made her, as by the pressure of a spring, give him a look that seemed to tell of things she couldn't speak. But she at last tried for one of them. "Oh it's you, father, who are what I call beyond everything. Nothing can pull *you* down." (496)

We can read this exchange as revealing, by its denial, of Adam Verver's repressed jealously, if we want. This would be, however, a subtlety of which the character is incapable. Another option available to us is to read it as his testimony to never having loved, really, either of his wives. This is certainly true, as we know from early on in the novel. He "brings in" Charlotte, as he always says, for his daughter's sake; Maggie need not worry about him. We even learn then that he is grateful for the timely death of his first wife just as the spirit of art collection descends on him, for he knows she would never have been able to accompany him in his new role as global connoisseur (109). I propose to read it, especially in light of Maggie's final response here, in a more absolute sense. Adam Verver is a visionary captain of industry and great art collector because *he is not capable* of the most intense and deepest kind of love. He may not be capable, if we take him with full seriousness, of any kind of love at all.

This form of being "beyond everything," as Maggie turns her epithet around on her father to distract him from the full import of his self-betrayal, strikes the true note of American madness. As we have seen in earlier chapters, especially in Ralph Waldo Emerson's case in "Experience" (1844), the most representative American visionary is "beyond everything." When Emerson admits that despite his expectation that his son's death would introduce him into reality by its sharpness and permanently wounding nature, and he experiences instead nothing worse than if he had lost some property, Emerson is testifying to being beyond love, if not incapable of it. Moreover, when a few paragraphs later in this essay Emerson celebrates the approach of some "new, yet unapproachable America" that he has discovered in the West, he characterizes this visionary America with attributes taken from around the globe and from different periods of history. America is the catachresis of the abysmal love of which the Emersonian visionary is not capable, except as a sublime image encountered in his experience of reading or thinking alone. James has already presented Adam Verver's discovery of his supreme idea of connoisseurship (109), which applies the aesthetic principle to his life as a whole and so disguises the split in him between commercial and cultural halves under the mask of pure acquisition of its own sake. In doing so, James shows his character as being a true Emersonian visionary (much like his own father), even as Verver analogizes this vision in term of John Keats's sonnet, "On First Looking Into Chapman's Homer," and his famous conceit of that experience being like proud Cortez discovering the Pacific, silent on a peak in Darien. (Of course, Verver repeats Keats's mistake, as James, too, must have known that it was Balboa who made this find, not Cortez.) However that may be, what we see in Verver is precisely the absence of the deepest love in the most representative form of American visionary experience.

As I have argued earlier, however, and find repeated here perfectly, is the contrasting kind of visionary experience, which is different in kind and degree of intensity. Maggie Verver, in a passage not cited above, admits to her father she is beyond everything, not knowing "where I am," as she puts it. In admitting this, she has the following experience: "The mere fine pulse of passion in [this love], the suggestion as of a creature consciously floating and shining in a warm summer sea, some element of dazzling sapphire and silver, a creature cradled upon depths, buoyant among dangers" (496)—this absolute experience of real love, of erotic rapture, even when it then sinks her in act to the bottom of the abyss of jealousy, is what she now knows her father never convinced anyone else, least of all himself, of being able to experience.

Such erotic rapture entails being vulnerable to wounding. When Maggie, a few pages later, realizes that without saying a word her father has decided to go back to American City with his young wife and thus save his daughter's and his own marriages, making his life and her life as successful as any work of art he has acquired, she experiences in her vulnerability what can only be called a strengthening and protective phallic jouissance:

> Before she knew it she was lifted aloft . . . in their transmuted union, to smile almost without pain. It was like a new confidence, and after another instant she knew ever still better why. Wasn't it because now also, on his side, he was thinking of her as his daughter, was *trying* her, during these mute seconds, as the child of his blood? It swelled in her fairly; it raised her higher, higher: she wasn't in that case a failure either—hadn't been, but the contrary; his strength was her strength, her pride was his, and they were decent and competent together. (540)

THE TRUTH OF AMERICAN MADNESS

In this scene we have the true climax of *The Golden Bowl*. After Maggie and Adam confess their belief in each other beyond all others, the halves of what I have termed Emersonian and Jamesian experiences of vision, of being beyond everything in the two opposing senses of psychotic narcissism and absolute abjection, respectively, are momentarily intermingled, if not fused, in ultimate intimacy: "His hands came out, and while her own took them he drew her to his breast and held her. He held her hard and kept her long, and she let herself go; but it was an embrace that, august and almost stern, produced for all its intimacy no revulsion and broke into no inconsequence of tears" (505).

What precedents can we raise for this momentous union? The union of Athena and Zeus? She pops out of his forehead after he has ripped the child out his sister-wife Hera's womb and swallows it whole so that no greater deity than he will be born into the world (power tops wisdom every time for the Greeks, it would seem). The Satanic version of this mythic scene of terrible self-begetting, as John Milton gives it, in the birth of Sin in *Paradise Lost*? There is Emerson's self-birth in "Experience," via the agency of his discovery of the "new, yet unapproachable America," as if the black hole of his son's death had turned into a worm hole of a new life, his father's life. Emerson imagines himself reborn after his son's death by sublime reading or thinking in imagery quite explicitly natal. Plate 100 in William Blake's *Jerusalem* (1804), of one hundred years before *The Golden Bowl*, also works, perhaps best of all. It shows Jerusalem as a young, naked woman being embraced by an old man in silk robes, Urthona (or Los, the creative principle of the redeemed human form divine), who here represents Albion (or the One Man). This statuesque archetypal figure is modeled on the conventional imagine of Jehovah, but with the distinctive Blakean twist: clearly visible female breasts! I bring in Blake, because James's late fiction especially, whether mediated by his father's writings or not, returns to the topoi of romanticism and plays them out compellingly.

However that may be, I think Alain Badiou's theory of the truth event and of the truth procedures to follow the event can work here best of all to clarify this scene. What reveals itself in this climactic vision is both the American madness and its cure appearing contingently as the event of truth in the love lives of this father-daughter pair. In other words, the truth of the American madness in *The Golden Bowl* lies not in Emersonian value alone, or in Jamesian self-abjecting love alone, but in their occasional abysmal moments of ultimate intimacy. To remain faithful to this vision of the truth event of love means these moments must remain occasional and contingent, and not try to become permanent.

The ritual of Maggie and her father meeting three times over the course of the novel can help us in this context. They meet alone together to decide to bring Charlotte into their lives. The two of them decide to go to Fawns rather than abroad, so that Maggie and Charlotte can face each other and Maggie disavow any jealousy; and, as noted in the quote above, they decide to separate for good. These three ritual-like meetings have the air of casting a magic spell when we think of them in retrospect, but in the actual reading they come up in the narrative as circumstances warrant. And they certainly don't mark permanence so much as change. They are, in fact, a therapeutic distancing of both father and daughter from the emotionally incestuous relationship. Such occasions of both growing separation and renewed fidelity to their relationship mark the truth-procedure process as Badiou explains it, and as I have detailed in earlier chapters.

I have also argued, following Klossowski on Nietzsche, that in reading we encounter consciously the otherwise unconscious experience of our impulsive drives—one after another or two dominant ones simultaneously in antagonistic contest—as they attempt to take hold of and use as allegorical masks, the *Stimmung*—the mood or tone or sounding—inscribed in the literary text, so that they may become fixed ideas and consume our lives with their madnesses. The word that signals the presence of this contest of drives in James's text is *vibration*. While not as pervasive as *anxiety* or as ubiquitous as *truth,* in *The Golden Bowl* the word *vibration* and its evident avatars *sound* pointedly, and often poignantly. The characters we have any interior vantage on—Maggie, Amerigo, Fanny—repeatedly suffer this "vibration," often, like Amerigo at the novel's opening, as a form of restlessness. Maggie describes such "nerves" as "the little idol of anxiety" (361), which gives rise to usually failed attempts to name and define this "vibration." The novel's second volume, for example, opens with Maggie finally confounding her husband's and mother-in-law's expectations, and Maggie envisions a huge porcelain pagoda silently looming in the middle of the garden of the lovers' lives. She now has simply knocked on it, and has received in answer to her quietly echoing tap a sharper sounding from within (303 ff.). Unable to do anything but employ words and images as components of catachresis for the otherwise unnamable experience of the drives, James's characters, as we read them mirroring our reading experience, repeatedly come face to face with what, with reference to her husband and Charlotte's adulterous relationship, Maggie calls "the figured void" (508). James pauses to remark and elaborate:

> There had been, through life, as we know, few quarters in which the Princess's fancy could let itself loose; but it shook off restraint when it plunged into the figured void of the detail of that relation. This was a realm it could people with images—again and again with fresh ones; they swarmed there like the strange combinations that lurked in the woods at twilight, they loomed into the definite and faded into the vague, their main present sign for her being however that they were always, that they were duskily, agitated. (508)

These images that yet fresh images beget are what Klossowski calls phantasms; these are the foundational elements of the simulacra the impulsive drives use to stabilize themselves so as to signal their passions. We combine and organize these simulacra into the admittedly phantasmagoric ideas of our imaginations of ourselves and of the world. When we can shake off our restraints in confronting the figured void of some previously unaccounted for and provocatively wounding new event, we then people that void with our visions, which otherwise convention and habit cover over and contain. Our new glimpses and procedures for remaining faithful to the new truths we have glimpsed keep our visions alive. Once again, our reading of the climactic father-daughter embrace concluding chapter 3 of book 5 is a good case in point. There, the aesthetic principle of vision represented by her father and the principle of love by his daughter momentarily fuse or interpenetrate in an ultimate form of intimacy that Blake, to recall him one again for clarification's sake, imagines as love making from head to toe.

What makes the novel's final scene so resonant, however, a kind of after-climax (and so perhaps a sign of feminine jouissance) is that it exhibits at once the subject of truth's exaltation and abjection. We see both this daughter's continuing abjection in the wild speculation of her abysmal love for Amerigo ("She had thrown the dice, but his hand was over the cast" [573]) and her lineage. She faces, for a moment, the tragic recognition of Amerigo's abject love for her emerging right there before her eyes, in outright disavowal of Charlotte's power to captivate any longer his gaze:

> He tried, too clearly, to please her—to meet her in her own way [about how useful Charlotte has been and will still be]; but with the result only that, close to her, her face kept before him, his hands holding her shoulders, his whole act enclosing her, he presently echoed: "See? I see nothing but *you*." And the truth of it had with this force after a moment so strangely lighted his eyes that as for pity and dread of them she buried her own in his breast. (574)

Maggie Verver experiences here the physical transport of married love, and its often awful costs.

Such tragic love is itself visionary, but as she says herself, it is "beyond everything," and so, beyond coherent or complete representation. It is what Lacan would call the real of the system of representation: that which is in it but not of it, also then "outside" it, and which the Symbolic Order would contain by its chain of signification, as in a game of hot potato, and which the imaginary would freeze into its purely reflective phantasms. It may be that the Princess wants "a happiness without a hole in it big enough for you to poke in your finger," or "a brilliant perfect surface" as Fanny Assingham glosses her desire—"the golden bowl," Maggie completes Fanny's reading for her, "as it was to have been." But "the golden bowl with all our happiness in it," the "bowl without the crack" (462), as Maggie learns, would enclose within its luminous void of feminine jouissance the truth of the American madness. As such, *The Golden Bowl*, I conclude, is Henry James's modern epic of reading in our global America, worth to stand beside the traditional epics of Homer, Virgil, Dante, and Milton.

appendix

WHY BADIOU COUNTS—
IN THIS BOOK AND GENERALLY

Several of my closest friends have repeatedly questioned why I use Alain Badiou in my recent work. Since they are all thoughtful people, and despite my best past efforts to explicate Badiou for my purposes, I am here making another attempt to explain why Badiou counts. I realize that this is a bit unorthodox, but if readers want to do so, they can just ignore it.

I choose this word *counts* with deliberate irony, of course, as the biggest objection to Badiou concerns his use of mathematics, specifically in *Being and Event* (2005) and its sequel, *Logics of Worlds* (2009), set theory and category theory, respectively. Both his ontology and phenomenology are thereby formalized in mathematical terms. Although there is a long tradition of doing so in both analytic and continental philosophy traditions, indeed going all the way back to Plato, most philosophers in recent years have not done so, and certainly the philosophers thought of as poststructuralist are generally not known for this mode of formalization. Jacques Lacan, the anti-philosopher, is the exception to this, as to all rules.

Badiou, in short, is doing something in his work that is largely unfamiliar nowadays and for humanists unwelcome. They cannot understand the mathematics, or, if they do, they believe mathematics as the discipline for formalizing philosophy works more reductively than does anthropology, history, psychoanalysis, sociology, politics, or linguistics. All modes of formalization, of course, are reductive and have the same two goals: to limit the everyday habits of mind that too often interfere with critical thinking and to make possible the communication of the practice of philosophy from one generation to the next.

Badiou chooses to use mathematics because his ontological insight is that being itself is mathematical, that is, being is the multiple to infinity. The expanse of being is infinitudes upon infinitudes of multiple. There is no closure and no single identity, no One—except as we humans construct it after the fact for our purposes. Given this ontology, every situation—a term Badiou derives more from the French tradition of mathematical theory than from John-Paul Sartre—is necessarily a political situation in which some human beings get to determine what counts as the one of the situation—that is, its identity and the select members of the situation, drawn from all its elements, that in turn count. These elements are members of the situation because they count toward its identity. They are so determined by those who say what counts in the count—the repetitive inventory—that they have set up regular procedures for so counting. Knowledge, in this context, tends to become encyclopedic and self-reinforcing. For Badiou, it is purely operational: it pertains to what makes the count count—an archive of taxonomies for identifying what matters.

Beyond such mathematical ontology and pragmatist epistemology, however, is Badiou's subtractive theory of truth. Truth is an event—fugitive and fleeting—that supplements any situation as counted by the state of the situation. This state of the situation is the present condition of the chronic inventory of the situation's approved membership. Imagine a perpetual census-taking. A truth emerges from within the situation as its founding void: a repressed or disavowed, unnamed or misnamed element of the situation that in fact forms the basis of the situation—on the analogy of the way the null set forms the basis of any set. Truth irrupts as what the situation has disavowed, and does so as something "real" exploding (as it supplements) the state of the situation. If we remember how the power set of any set contains more subsets than there are original elements in the set, we can begin to see, I think, the fertility of set theory for Badiou's allegory of truth.

By naming this truth, the subject—which for Badiou is never simply individual but always determined by a collective project—inaugurates a new configuration of the situation upon the ruins of the old. A revolutionary truth is one in which this truth precludes the coercive forcing of the new configuration upon all elements of the situation, so that a new situation can emerge cleanly, the way a new category does, from the truth procedures set up by the subject of this truth, not as a new repressive law but rather as an experimental test of the universality of the truth in question. The four primary domains in which truths emerge or manifest themselves for Badiou as new beings in the world are politics, science, art, and love. Philosophy invents no new truths, but instead analyzes, evaluates, and coordinates the truths emerging from these domains.

Although I have read all of Badiou available in French and English, as well as his many commentators and critics, I find that of the former, Peter Hallward, in *Badiou: A Subject to Truth* (Minneapolis: University of Minnesota Press, 2003), is the most helpful, explaining, for instance, the thirty-eight meanings of "subtraction" in Badiou; and of the latter, Slavoj Žižek in *In Defense of Lost Causes* (New York: Verso, 2008) is most provocative, for instance, in raising the questions of capitalism's inherently transformative dynamic and its outmoding effects on the idea and reality of class. Because Žižek does not deal with Badiou's mathematics, however, he fails to understand that the state of the situation under capitalism or under Rome counts as zero, as null set, as part of the void, the class of its elements that will not count as members. The state of the situation, that is, already subtracts into the void the class that does not count: illegal immigrants, for example. The critic, the philosopher, is then to subtract from this subtraction in helping to name the nameless with a name already subtracted from the field of positively recognized names and not already in circulation as part of the official story of reality. By using Badiou in this book I hope to begin this process of revisionary naming with critical reading in American studies.

Besides my friends' objection to Badiou's mathematical ontology and eventful theory of truth, they argue that I can simply use the work of literary figures in the romantic tradition—Blake, Shelley, Yeats, etc.—to make the points I want to make, or indeed the points that Badiou makes. Sometimes, these same friends go further and say that I should not bother with reading through the texts of any figures as so many masks or personae of my own message when I can even more simply just speak in my own person and elaborate my position, as it were, *ex cathedra*.

The reason I do what I do—produce theory via reading the texts of others—is that I am in my criticism, well, a critic. That is, I am a scholarly reader of and commentator upon texts. I am not Immanuel Kant, nor was I meant to be. My mind as a critic, such as it is, is itself a text made up of all the other texts I have read. Theory is the name for the order I can bring to those memories, and the names of the theorists are the presiding *genius loci* of the admittedly odd commonplaces of my mind. In this context, Badiou is the present name for the visionary power of the romantic tradition, even as he would contend he is a classicist—both Platonic and Pascalian—and is harshly critical of German romanticism. But, thanks to Freud and Harold Bloom, we know that story all too well by now. If under the guise of such a figure as Badiou I can insinuate the romantic tradition of imagination and thinking into our discussions, so much the better, as I do not believe, regardless of what my friends say, we can convince contemporaries to take seriously that tradition for our time. However, I will conclude with an explicit bow to and endorsement of that tradition—for my friends' sakes.

In Blake's *Milton,* one of the recurring mythic tropes is that of the secret moment in each day that Satan's watch-fiends can never find and inventory. This is the creative moment when a vision can arise that is a poetic event: spontaneous, unpredictable, and transformative. This is so only if it is not strangled as it is born by the habits of conventional thinking.

This idea of the fugitive, creative moment is central to Blake, and indeed to all the romantics, and in the terms in which I have stated it, it is easy to dismiss as outmoded, a pious relic of a defeated, liberal humanist past, and yet, for me, it remains one of the most significant truths there is. Badiou's philosophy is, in this context, an ironic visionary allegory for the propagation of faith in the transformative power of the creative moment that can escape the mindless inventory of Satan's watch-fiends. Upon such moments, worlds can turn. Or at the least, heads.

notes

preface

1. Henry James, *Complete Stories, 1892–1898,* ed. Edward W. Said (New York: Library of America, 1996), 347.
2. Ralph Waldo Emerson, *Essays and Lectures,* ed. Joel Porte (New York: Library of America, 1983), 424.

introduction

1. See Erich Auerbach, *Mimesis: The Representation of Reality in Western Literature,* trans. Willard R. Trask (Princeton, NJ: Princeton University Press, 1953, 2003), 353.
2. See Pierre Klossowski, *Nietzsche and the Vicious Circle,* trans. Daniel W. Smith (Chicago: The University of Chicago Press, 1969), 41.
3. Friedrich Nietzsche, *The Gay Science with a Prelude in German in Rhymes and an Appendix of Songs,* ed. Bernard Williams, trans. Josefine Nauckhoff and Andrian Del Caro (New York: Cambridge University Press, 2002), 190–91.
4. My reading is influenced here by a forthcoming essay in *boundary 2* from Hans Ulrich Gumbrecht, "Reading for the *Stimmung*? About the Ontology of Literature Today."
5. Cited in Quentin Anderson, *The Imperial Self: An Essay in American Literary and Cultural History* (New York: Vintage Books, 1971).

chapter 1

1. For Smith's biography, see Karen L. Hellekson, *The Science Fiction of Cordwainer Smith* (Jefferson, NC: McFarland and Co., Inc., 2001), 5–6.
2. To note just two of these recent books, see Christ Hables Gray, *Cyborg Citizen* (New York: Routledge, 2001), and Francis Fukuyama, *Our Posthuman Future: Consequences of the Biotechnology Revolution* (New York: Farrar, Strauss and Giroux, 2002). Fukuyama is particularly good at separating realistic from purely imaginary expectations with respect to these consequences. His own ultimate practical solution to the dilemmas they inspire, conservative populist that he is, is

to remind us of the power of the ballot box, which, given his very own call for the new international controls and institutions in these matters, leads only to further dilemmas, it would seem.

3. Elaine L. Graham, *Representatives of the Post/Human: Monsters, Aliens and Others in Popular Culture* (New Brunswick, NJ: Rutgers University Press, 2002). Hereafter, this work is cited parenthetically in the text by page number. Graham argues for writing the term as "post/human" (rather than any other way), and in discussing her work I use that same term, but "post-human" elsewhere in my writing. I have also used other people's preferred usage when citing their own work. For a recent study that discusses in more detail the cybernetic connection to the "post/human," see N. Katherine Hayles, *How We Became Posthuman: Virtual Bodies in Cybernetics, Literature and Informatics* (Chicago: University of Chicago Press, 1999).

4. Fukuyama's book takes a very different theoretical approach to erecting a critical framework than Graham's, as we shall shortly see. Fukuyama vainly resurrects a scholastic version of Aristotle's conception of human nature and then attempts to supplement its perceived inadequacies with some mumbo jumbo from modern statistical research. The result is the production of a truly "monstrous" version of typical or representative human nature intended to be appropriate for so-called liberal capitalist democracies. This "creation" of Fukuyama's is stranger than any Mary Shelley envisioned.

5. See Martin Heidegger, "The Question Concerning Technology" and "Building, Dwelling, Thinking," both in *Basic Writings,* ed. David Farrell Krell (London: Routledge, 1993).

6. For one of the more influential versions of this reading of Foucault, see Arnold I. Davidson, "Archeology, Genealogy, Ethics," in *Foucault: A Critical Reader,* ed. David Couzens Hoy (Oxford: Blackwell, 1986), 221–34.

7. See my *Radical Parody: American Culture and Critical Agency after Foucault* (New York: Columbia University Press, 1992).

8. These essays, in revised form, constitute what will be the core of Bové's forthcoming study on Adams for Harvard University Press.

9. For a brief influential discussion of "the inhuman," see Jean-François Lyotard.

10. For his latest discussion on the topic, see Jacques Derrida, "Hostipitality" [sic], in *Acts of Religion,* ed. Gil Anidjar (New York: Routledge, 2002), 356–420.

11. See Arkady Plotnitsky, *The Knowable and the Unknowable: Modern Science, Nonclassical Thought, and the "Two Cultures"* (Ann Arbor: University of Michigan Press, 2002).

12. See "Planet-Buyer and Cat-Master" in my *Empire Burlesque: The Fate of Critical Culture in Global America* (Durham, NC: Duke University Press, 2003).

13. For one exemplary remembrance, see Geoffrey Hartman, "Language and Culture after the Holocaust," in *The Fateful Question of Culture* (New York: Columbia University Press, 1997), 99–140.

14. Cordwainer Smith, *Nostrilia* (Framingham, MA: The NESFA Press, 1994), 128. This is one of Smith's own poems, in this case about the mysterious alien race of "Daimoni" that came and went, *apparently* leaving scarcely a trace of their divinely obvious selves.

15. For a more sustained imaginative version of this untimely "human, all-too-human" Nietzschean critical gesture of mine, see Kenzaburo Oe's stunningly ironic rereading of Blake's influence on his life and work, *Rouse Up O Young Men of the*

New Age! Trans. and with an afterword by John Nathan (New York: Grove Press, 2002).

16. Alain Badiou, *Being and Event,* trans. Oliver Feltham (New York: Continuum, 2005). Hereafter, this work is cited parenthetically by page number.

chapter 2

1. Peter Hallward, *Badiou: A Subject to Truth* (Minneapolis: University of Minnesota Press, 2003). This is the best introduction to Badiou available in English. I have drawn heavily upon it for my summary of his position. For the disciplinary basis of Badiou's version of set theory, see Paul Cohen, *Set Theory and the Continuum Hypothesis* (New York: W. A. Benjamin, 1966).
2. Alain Badiou, *Saint Paul: The Foundation of Universalism,* trans. Ray Brassier (Stanford, CA: Stanford University Press, 2003).
3. Alain Badiou, *Theoretical Writings,* trans. and ed. Ray Brassier and Alberto Toscano (New York: Continuum, 2004).
4. *The Fundamentalism Project* consists of five substantial tomes, all edited by Martin E. Marty and R. Scott Appleby (et al.) and published by the University of Chicago Press from 1991 through 1995. All volumes are now in paperback. The titles of the individual volumes are: *Fundamentalisms Observed,* vol. 1; *Fundamentalisms and Society: Reclaiming the Sciences, the Family, and Education,* vol. 2; *Fundamentalisms and the State: Remaking Polities, Economies, and Militance,* vol. 3; *Accounting for Fundamentalisms: The Dynamic Character of Movements,* vol. 4; and *Fundamentalisms Comprehended,* vol. 5. An early selection of the contributions dealing with Islam was edited by James Piscatori and was published in 1991 by the American Academy of Arts and Sciences as *Islamic Fundamentalisms and the Gulf Crisis.* The entire project was underwritten by a substantial MacArthur Foundation grant. I am indebted to these volumes for whatever understanding of the topic I have. I am also indebted to Paul A. Bové for pointing me in their direction at an early stage in the research for this chapter.
5. For this term and the explanation of its usage, see the general editors' conclusion, "Remaking the State: The Limits of the Fundamentalist Imagination," in *Fundamentalisms and the State,* vol. 3 of *The Fundamentalism Project,* 620–44.
6. See Robin Griffith-Jones, *The Gospel According to Paul: The Creative Genius Who Brought Jesus to the World* (San Francisco: HarperSanFrancisco, 2004).
7. See James L. Peacock and Tim Pettyjohn, "Fundamentalisms Narrated: Muslim, Christian, and Mystical," in *Fundamentalisms Comprehended,* vol. 5 of *The Fundamentalism Project,* 115–34.
8. See Shadia B. Drury, *Leo Strauss and the American Right* (New York: St. Martin's Press, 1997).
9. The entire final volume of *The Fundamentalism Project, Fundamentalisms Comprehended,* is devoted to these explanations.
10. See Griffith-Jones, *The Gospel According to Paul,* 479–500.
11. Badiou, *Saint Paul,* 62–64.
12. Sigmund Freud, *The Schreber Case,* trans. Andrew Webber, with an introduction by Colin MacCabe (New York: Penguin Books, 2003).
13. Freud, *The Schreber Case,* 60.
14. All my citations of Elder Evans's conversion story come from Peacock and Pettyjohn, "Fundamentalisms Narrated," 115–34.

chapter 3

1. Alain Badiou, *Saint Paul: The Foundation of Universalism,* trans. Ray Brassier (Stanford, CA: Stanford University Press, 2003), 5. Hereafter, this work is cited parenthetically as *SP.*
2. Robin Griffith-Jones, *The Gospel According to Paul: The Creative Genius Who Brought Jesus to the World* (San Francisco: HarperSanFrancisco, 2004), 422–24. I have modified some of these more colloquial terms back into the traditional formulations when it has seemed to make for greater clarity for the general reader. I cite from this text because Griffith-Jones is a New Testament scholar of considerable reputation whose translations capture the concrete power of the original text.
3. Ibid., 426.
4. Frank Lentricchia and Jody McAuliffe, *Crimes of Art and Terror* (Chicago: University of Chicago Press, 2003), 3.
5. James Strachey, ed., *The Standard Editions of the Complete Psychological Works of Sigmund Freud,* vol. 20, *An Autobiographical Study, Inhibitions, Symptoms and Anxiety* (1925–26) (London: Hogarth Press), 1959.
6. See the "Historical Introduction" to Søren Kierkegaard, *The Concept of Anxiety, Kierkegaard Writings,* vol. 8, ed. and trans. Reidar Thornte (Princeton, NJ: Princeton University Press, 1980), vii–xviii.
7. Richard G. Heimber, Cynthia L. Turk, and Douglas S. Mennin, eds., *Generalized Anxiety Disorder: Advances in Research and Practice* (New York: Guilford Press, 2004). See, especially, Michel J. Dugas, Kristin Buhr, and Robert Ladouceur, "The Role of Intolerance of Uncertainty in Etiology and Maintenance," 143–63.
8. See Strachey, *The Standard Edition,* introduction to vol. 20, *An Autobiographical Study, Inhibitions, Symptoms and Anxiety,* 15.
9. Alain Badiou, "Lack and Destruction," *Umbr(a): A Journal of the Unconscious* 2 (2003): 42–43. Hereafter, this work is cited parenthetically as LD. Badiou focuses here on Lacan's remarks about anxiety from *The Seminar of Jacques Lacan, Book 1: Freud's Papers on Technique 1953–1954,* ed. Jacques-Alain Miller, trans. John Forrester (New York: Norton, 1988), and *The Seminar of Jacques Lacan, Book 11: The Four Fundamental Concepts of Psychoanalysis,* ed. Jacques-Alain Miller, trans. Alan Sheridan (New York: W. W. Norton, 1981). For an extended study of Lacan's views on anxiety, see Roberto Harari, *Lacan's Seminar on "Anxiety,"* with a foreword by Charles Shepherdson, trans. Jane C. Lamb-Ruiz, rev. and ed. Rico Frances (New York: Other Press, 2001).
10. Wallace Stevens, "An Ordinary Evening in New Haven, XII," in *Stevens: Collected Poetry and Prose,* ed. Frank Kermode and Joan Richardson (New York: Library of America, 1997), 404.
11. Slavoj Žižek, *Iraq: The Borrowed Kettle* (New York: Verso, 2004), 127.
12. Ibid.

chapter 4

1. For the basis of this view, see Jonathan Arac, *The Emergence of American Literary Narrative, 1820–1860* (Cambridge, MA: Harvard University Press, 2005).

2. Ralph Waldo Emerson, *Essays and Lectures* (New York: 1983), 167.

3. Leon Edel, ed., *The Letters of Henry James*, vol. 1, 1885–1872 (Cambridge, MA: Harvard Belknap Press, 1975), 102.

4. Henry James, *Literary Criticism*, vol. 2: *European Writers and Prefaces to the New York Edition* (New York: Library of America, 1983), 198.

5. See "Empire Baroque: Becoming Other in Henry James" in my *Empire Burlesque: The Fate of Critical Culture in Global America* (Durham, NC: Duke University Press, 2003).

6. William H. O'Donnell, ed., *Later Essays*, vol. VII (London: Palgrave Macmillan, 2002), 84. For "Emersonianism," see Donald E. Pease, "Emerson's 'Experience' and the Crisis in Emersonianism," forthcoming in *boundary 2*.

7. Robert Stone, *Prime Green: Remembering the Sixties* (New York: Houghton Mifflin, 2007), 153. Much of the vision here portrayed, Stone admits, derives from the influence of D. H. Lawrence's American writings, a subject to be explored subsequently.

chapter 5

1. The latest volume by Mick Foley is *The Hardcore Diaries* (New York: Pocket Books, 2007).

2. Alain Badiou, *Polemics*, trans. Steve Corcoran (London: Verso, 2006), 43. For a radically different view of 9/11, see Frank Lentricchia and Jody McAuliffe, *Crimes of Art and Terror* (Chicago: University of Chicago Press, 2003).

3. Alain Badiou, *Saint Paul: The Foundation of Universalism*, trans. Ray Brassier (Stanford, CA: Stanford University Press, 2003).

4. John Ashbery, *A Worldly Country: New Poems* (New York: Ecco Press, 2007).

5. Jacques Lacan, *Seminar, Livre XXIII: Le Sinthome, 1975–1976*, ed. Jacques Alain-Miller (Paris: Editions du Seuil, 2005), 17. The published English translation is partial and appeared in *Ornicar? (1976–77)*: 6–11. There is an unauthorized manuscript version of the complete *Seminar* in circulation as well based on texts established by Luke Thurston. I have also consulted these published and unpublished sources. For the best recent study of the Joycean dimension of *Seminar XXIII*, see Philip Dravers, "Joyce and the Sinthome: Aiming at the Fourth Term of the Knot," *Psychoanalytic Notebooks of the LSNLS* 13: "Lacan with Joyce," 1–25.

6. "The Beast in the Jungle," in *Tales of Henry James*, ed. Christof Wegelin and Henry B. Wonham (New York: Norton, 2003). The companion tale, "The Jolly Corner" (1908) tells the story of an expatriate American returning to New York City to take care of the final disposal of his properties there, including his childhood home. Spencer Brydon, the protagonist in question, becomes convinced that if he haunts the premises at midnight he will come upon the ghost of all that he never became, the crass commercial personality his aesthetic personality repressed. Here, the living man turns the tables on the undead one in ways that could easily lend themselves to a similar kind of symptomatic reading.

7. Joel Porte, ed., *Emerson: Essays and Lectures* (New York: Library of America, 1983).

8. Jonathan Lear, *Radical Hope: Ethics in the Face of Cultural Devastation* (Cambridge, MA: Harvard University Press, 2006).

9. Charles Taylor, "A Different Kind of Courage," *The New York Review of Books* 54 (April 26, 2007): 7, 22–26.
10. Wallace Stevens, *Collected Poems* (New York: Knopf, 1954, 2005).
11. Holly Stevens, ed., *The Letters of Wallace Stevens* (New York: Knopf, 1965), 549.

chapter 6

1. Erich Auerbach, *Mimesis: The Representation of Reality in Western Literature*, trans. Willard Trask with an introduction by Edward W. Said (Princeton: Princeton University Press, 2003).
2. Michael Sheringham, *Everyday Life: Theories and Practices from Surrealism to the Present* (New York: Oxford University Press, 2006).
3. John Cheever, *Falconer* (New York: Vintage, 1992).
4. John Ashbery, *Self-Portrait in a Convex Mirror: Poems* (New York: Penguin, 1990).
5. Charles Altieri, *Painterly Abstraction in Modernist American Poetry* (London: Cambridge University Press, 1990).
6. Ralph Waldo Emerson, *Essays and Lectures*, ed. Joel Porte (New York: Library of America, 1983).
7. Stanley Cavell, *This New yet Unapproachable America: Essays after Emerson after Wittgenstein*, Frederick Ives Carpenter Lectures, 1987 (New York: Living Batch Books, 1994).
8. Cordwainer Smith, *The Rediscovery of Man* (New York: NESFA Press, 1993).

chapter 7

1. The dates refer to original publications in magazines.
2. See James's *CS1-Complete Stories, 1864–1874* (New York: Library of America, 1999).
3. See James's *CS2-Complete Stories, 1884–1891* (New York: Library of America, 1999).
4. See Huguette Glowinski, Zita M. Marks, and Sara Murphy, *A Compendium of Lacanian Terms* (London: Free Association, 2001). For Lacan, *jouissance* takes two forms: phallic and feminine. The former would be perfectly exemplified in both stories by the sudden impulsive stabbing of the portraits, granting relief; the latter, in "The Liar," by Oliver Lyon's dizziness and prolonged excitement after he witnesses the scene of his masterpiece's orgiastic destruction. So-called "adult genital sexuality" versus "polymorphous perversity" would be the classic psychoanalytic way of putting this difference.
5. I am following the lead here of Quentin Anderson. See Anderson, *The American Henry James* (New Brunswick, NJ: Rutgers University Press, 1957).
6. Examples of James's levity are scattered throughout both stories. The woman's last name of "Everett" in the earlier story and the woman's first name of Everina in the later one are both names containing humankind's mythic first mother's notorious name of Eve. In "The Liar" the model of the type of portrait the artist wishes to emulate is "The Tailor," one of Giovanni Battista Moroni's mannerist

classics. The figure of the young man, the tailor of the title, is simultaneously so evidently a figure broadly suggestive of, but not specifically identified with, the figure of Pan. In this context of James being between realism and vision, I find this reference revealing for thinking about the form of James's art, here in the artist-tales but also more generally.

7. The most influential critic discussing the visionary imagination is, of course, Harold Bloom. A good overall introduction to his work is to be found in *Poetics of Influence*. See Bloom, *New and Selected Essays,* ed. and intro. John Hollander (New Haven, CT: Henry Schwab, 1988). Critics of James treat his visionary tendencies in terms of James's own famous distinction between realism and romance, about which I propose my own views in chapter 2 of *Lionel Trilling: The Work of Liberation (*Madison: University of Wisconsin Press, 1988).

8. Here is Luxon's introduction to this online edition of the text:

> The first edition of 1667 printed the poem in ten books. The Arguments at the head of each book were added in subsequent imprints of the first edition. In 1674, a fully "Revised and Augmented" edition with new front matter, arguments at the head of each book, and a new division into twelve books was issued. Milton scholars generally have used this edition as the standard for any new scholarly edition. The *Milton Reading Room* text of *Paradise Lost* was prepared from the copy of 1674 on University Microfilm's Wing 609–9* copy (Early English books, 1641–1700; 609:9), and checked against a copy of 1674 in the Rauner Special Collections Library at Dartmouth College. Whenever 1674 made no sense, the equivalent passage from 1667 (Wing 609–4) was checked and sometimes followed. All deviations from 1674 are recorded in the notes.

See Cordelia Zukerman and Thomas H. Luxon, Introduction, *Paradise Lost* by John Milton. The Milton Reading Room, Dartmouth College, February 14, 2007, http://www.dartmouth.edu/~milton/reading_room/pl/intro/index.shtml (accessed March 20, 2009).

9. See my *Empire Burlesque: The Fate of Cultural Criticism in Global America* (Durham, NC: Duke University Press, 2003). In "Empire Baroque: Becoming Other in Henry James," I elaborate on James's slippery nature and relate it to the specter of what I term global America (237–300). To be brief here by necessity, the figure of "the new, yet unapproachable America" that Emerson declares in "Experience" (1844) he manifestly discovers in the West as his visionary destiny, rather than avow any grief for his dead son and namesake. This "always already" death of love is the American form of Satan's sin. In this chapter, too, I assess the relative critical value of the work by Millicent Bell, Philip Horne, Ross Posnock, and John Carlos Rowe. Eric Savoy's readings of James (see his *Henry James and Queer Formalism,* forthcoming, Duke University Press, 2009), found often in the pages of this journal and composing the basis of his forthcoming study, provides for me the model of a contemporary critical approach that makes the most of both older and newer forms of scholarship in James studies.

chapter 8

1. Michel Foucault, *The Hermeneutics of the Subject: Lectures at the College de France 1981–1982,* ed. Francois Ewald and Alessandro Fontana, trans. Graham

Burchell (New York: Palgrave Macmillan, 2005).

2. Henry James, *The Portrait of a Lady: A Norton Critical Edition*, 2d ed., ed. Robert O. Bamberg (New York: W. W. Norton, 1995). Hereafter, this work is cited parenthetically by page number only.

3. Foucault, *The Hermeneutics of the Subject*, 308.

4. Ibid.

5. W. B. Yeats, *The Collected Works, Volume 1: The Poems*, rev. ed. Richard J. Finnegan (New York: Scribner's, 1997), 190.

6. James Baldwin, *Blues for Mister Charlie: A Play* (1964; repr., New York: Vintage International, 1992).

7. Ibid., 32.

8. Chapter 9 is a more in-depth discussion of this topic.

9. See Pierre Klossowski, *Nietzsche and the Vicious Circle*, trans. Daniel W. Smith (Chicago: University of Chicago Press, 1997).

10. Foucault, *The Hermeneutics of the Subject*, 282, 284–85.

11. For what is still the best study of this work in relation to Blake's poetic mythology, see Northrop Frye, *Fearful Symmetry: A Study of William Blake* (1947; repr., Princeton, NJ: Princeton University Press, 1972).

12. Baldwin, *Blues for Mister Charlie*, 1–2.

13. Lionel Trilling, "Princess Casamassima," in *The Moral Obligation to Be Intelligent*, ed. with an intro. Leon Wieseltier (New York: Farrar, Strauss and Giroux, 2001), 149–77.

14. Ibid., 152.

15. James Baldwin, *The Amen Corner: A Play* (New York: Vintage International, 1968).

chapter 9

1. I allude here to the psychoanalytically inspired literary and cultural studies of such critics as Christopher Lane, Tim Dean, Joan Copjec, Jean-Michel Rabate, Charles Shepherdson, Leo Bersani, Julia Kristeva, and Slavoj Žižek, among others, including Donald E. Pease. Although not all of those I just mentioned (or am thinking of) do gay studies or queer theory, much of the most important and promising work is being done there, and all of the promising studies bear witness to these developments.

2. W. B. Yeats, *Per Amica Silentia Lenae*, in *The Collected Works of W. B. Yeats, Volume V: Later Essays*, ed. William H. O'Donnell (New York: Scribner's, 1994), 9. Hereafter, this work is cited parenthetically by page number only.

3. Slavoj Žižek, *Enjoy Your Symptom: Jacques Lacan in Hollywood and Out*, 2d ed. (New York: Routledge, 2001), 200.

4. Ibid.

5. Ibid.

6. James Purdy, *63: Dream Palace and Other Stories* (New York: Penguin Books, 1980). This book was first published in 1957 by New Directions under the title *The Color of Darkness*.

7. James Purdy, *The Candles of Your Eyes and Thirteen Other Stories* (San Francisco: City Lights, 1991), 22.

8. Christopher Lane, "Out with James Purdy: An Interview," the James Purdy Society Web site, http://www.wright.edu/~martin.kich/PurdySoc/Lane.htm. The

interview was recorded on November 27, 1993. Hereafter, this work is cited parenthetically by page number only. Page numbers refer to this online version printed from the Web site.

9. James Purdy, *Proud Flesh: Four Short Plays* (Northridge, CA: Lord John Press, 1980), 19.

10. Ibid., 18.

11. James Purdy, *Moe's Villa and Other Stories* (New York: Carroll and Graf, 2004), 178. Subsequent references to this text are cited parenthetically by page number only.

conclusion

1. Henry James, *The Golden Bowl,* with an Introduction by Denis Donoghue (London: Everyman Library, Knopf , 1992).

index

Abraham and Isaac, 22–23
Alger, Horatio, Jr., 76
The Amen Corner (Baldwin), 130–31
America, 54; 9/11, 78, 83, 85–87, 91, 95, 133, 138–39; and abjection, 81–82, 85; and Abu Ghraib, 58; American Dream, 79; culture of security, 134, 139, 141; exceptionalism, viii, 86; manifest destiny, 75; Renaissance, 73; sci-fi culture, ix; the West, 76. See also global America; subject
Another Country (Baldwin), 129
anxiety, 63–65, 133–34, 158
Ashbery, John, 86, 106. See also *Self-Portrait in a Convex Mirror*
Auerbach, Erich, x, 1–4, 6, 101–2, 106. See also *Mimesis*
The Auroras of Autumn (Stevens), 95–96

Badiou, Alain, ix, x, 5, 7, 31, 33–34, 38–44, 46, 55, 57, 64–69, 83–86, 99, 118, 157, 161–64; and Heidegger, 42. See also *Being and Event; Logics of Worlds; Saint Paul: The Foundations of Universalism*
Baldwin, James, xi, 9. See also *The Amen Corner; Another Country; Blues for Mister Charlie;* "Sonny's Blues"
"The Beast in the Jungle" (James), x, 87–91

Being and Event (Badiou), 31, 36, 161
Blake, William, 75, 78, 138, 142, 157, 159, 163–64; Kenzaburo Oe's rereading of, 166n15; and the "State," 79. See also *The Book of Thel*
Bloom, Harold, 103, 164, 171n7
Blues for Mister Charlie (Baldwin), 125, 127–29
The Book of Thel (Blake), 53, 127
Bourdieu, Pierre: "habitus," 79
Bové, Paul, 21, 99, 166n8
"Brawith" (Purdy), 138, 142–49
Bush, George Walker, 85; and the "War on Terror," 44, 127; and pre-millennial fundamentalism, 47; on Iraq, 79

Cheever, John, 106. See also *The Falconer*
Clearing the Forest (Purdy), 141
Crimes of Art and Terror (Lentricchia and McAuliffe), 62

Derrida, Jacques, 22
drive, 91; definition of, 86

Emerson, Ralph Waldo, x, 6, 10–11, 73–80, 87, 91, 103–5, 107, 155, 157
Empire Burlesque (O'Hara), 82–83, 171n9
Enjoy Your Symptom (Žižek), 134–36

INDEX

The Falconer (Cheever), x, 99–102
Foucault, Michel, xi, 9, 17, 21, 23–24, 26, 32–33; "disciplinary practice," 79. See also *The Hermeneutics of the Subject*
Freud, Sigmund, 78, 99, 138, 140, 164; on Dr. Schreber, 51–33, 88; see also *Inhibitions, Symptoms, and Anxiety*
Fukuyama, Francis, 165n2, 166n4
fundamentalism, viii, ix, 5, 45–48, 50–51, 52–54, 138

global America , viii, 5, 7, 11, 73–76, 83, 86–87, 121
The Golden Bowl (James), vii, x, xi, 150–60
Graham, Elaine L., 16, 23–29, 166n3, 166n4
Gumbrecht, Hans Ulrich, x, 3, 165n4

Haraway, Donna, 17, 24–26
Hegel, Georg Wilhelm Friedrich: "spirit of the age," 79
Heidegger, Martin, 18–21, 23, 31, 42, 63, 84, 99
The Hermeneutics of the Subject (Foucault), 120, 122–24, 126

identity, x, 4, 10, 28–29, 49–51, 57, 61, 76, 137, 142, 162; identity-theme, 57, 83, 95; of groups, 58; in politics, viii, 91, 93; and self-revision, 19, 21. See also truth procedures
Inhibitions, Symptoms, and Anxiety (Freud), 63
In Defense of Lost Causes (Žižek), 163
In Search of Lost Time (Proust), 100

James, Henry, x, xi, 6, 7, 11, 76–78, 101, 107, 111, 170n6, 171n7. See also "The Beast in the Jungle"; *The Golden Bowl*; "The Jolly Corner"; "The Liar"; *The Portrait of a Lady*; *The Sacred Fount*; "The Story of a Masterpiece"
"The Jolly Corner" (James), 169n6

Judeo-Christian tradition, 19, 23

Kant, Immanuel, 164
Keats, John, 93, 156
Kierkegaard, Søren, 22, 63
Klossowski, Pierre, 3–5, 9, 158

Lacan, Jacques, ix, x, 7, 32, 41–42, 55, 83, 85, 133, 140–41, 160–61; and definition of *sinthome*, 134; and jouissance, x, xi, 7, 11, 87, 113–15, 118, 133–35, 140, 156, 160, 170n4; and *le sinthome*, x, xi, 6, 33, 86–87, 90–91, 134–37, 142–43, 149; and the three orders, 29, 42, 45, 48–49, 52–53, 57–58, 60–61, 66–67, 69, 87, 90, 133, 135, 145, 160. See also the real; *Seminar 23: Le Sinthome*
"The Liar" (James), 111–18
Logics of Worlds (Badiou), 161

de Man, Paul, 6, 37
Mimesis (Auerbach), 97–99

Nietzsche, Friedrich, 3–5, 7–10, 18, 21, 23, 84, 138–39; and *amor fati*, xi, 78, 120, 126–27, 130–31; and eternal return, 9; and the "Last Man," 139; and *ressentiment*, 48
nihilism, 21, 85

Pease, Donald, 11, 79, 139
The Portrait of a Lady (James), 120–21
post/human, vii, viii, 16–7, 19–20, 22, 24, 27, 153; and the cyborg, the cyborg, 25; as Übermensch, 4, 9; and the nonhuman, 22–23
public intellectuals, 5, 28, 77, 83, 163–64
Purdy, James, x, xi, 6, 9, 132–34, 136–39; interview with Christopher Lane, 140–41. See also *Clearing the Forest*; "Brawith"

Radical Hope: Ethics in the Face of Cultural Devastation (Lear), 91–95

reading, xi; American difference of, viii; experience of, vii; and self-interpretation, viii; and truth procedures, 6
the Real, ix, xi, 5, 35, 138, 141, 143, 149
Romanticism, 157, 164

The Sacred Fount (James), 113
Said, Edward, 99, 102
Saint Paul: The Foundations of Universalism (Badiou), 50, 55, 58, 68
Self-Portrait in a Convex Mirror (Ashbery), x, 102, 105–6
Seminar 23: Le Sinthome (Lacan), 86
Smith, Cordwainer, 15–16, 29–30, 166n14
"Sonny's Blues" (Baldwin), 129
Stevens, Wallace, 10, 68, 103. See also *The Auroras of Autumn*
Stoicism, 33, 120, 124, 126
"The Story of a Masterpiece" (James), 111–18
Strauss, Leo, 47–48
subject, 38, 122–24, 141, 151; American, ix, 86, 102, 105–6, 127, 131, 151–53, 155; and anxiety, 65–67; modern, 19, 101; and psychoanalysis, 43, 133, 153; and revision, 18–19; and truth, 6, 19, 32, 36, 42–43, 50, 55–61, 69

sublime, 87, 91, 125

terrorism, ix, 5, 61–62, 64, 66, 68–69, 81, 91, 127, 139
truth, 84, 158; as correspondence, 31–22; the four domains of, 86; procedures, 6, 34, 37, 59, 86, 157, 159; and set theory, 39–43, 84–85, 162; as unveiling, 31; and the void, 34–35, 39, 46, 53, 61, 85, 119, 159
The Twilight of the Idols (Nietzsche), 21

vision: culture of, 134, 139; visionary experience, 155–57; visionary imagination, 132–33, 139, 149, 171n7

Whitman, Walt, 10, 103
will-to-power, 9, 18–19, 21; and Heidegger's will-to-will, 18–21, 27–29
Wordsworth, William, 80, 133

Yeats, William Butler, 78, 124–25, 132–34, 138, 140, 163

Žižek, Slavoj, 12, 69. See also *Enjoy Your Symptom; In Defense of Lost Causes*

www.ingramcontent.com/pod-product-compliance
Lightning Source LLC
Chambersburg PA
CBHW020800160426
43192CB00006B/397